Ruby's Son

A journey from poverty to peace
By BOBBY LANGLEY

Edited and arranged by Mark Cook

Beasley Town Press
1114 Culpepper Circle
Franklin, Tenn. 37064

In Loving Memory
This book is dedicated to my mother and father
Ruby Irene Hammox Langley
Tyree Eugene Langley

and to my brothers and sisters
William Eugene Langley
Hubert Lee Langley
John Tyree (J.T.) Langley
Mary Clair Langley
Carolyn Ann Langley
Ronnie Merrill Langley

"I can do all things through Christ who strengthens me."
Philippians 4:13

An aerial photo from the early 1950s shows the north part of the Battle Ground Academy campus. The view is to the northeast. Granbury Street and the shotgun shacks of Beasley Town can be seen just beyond the fence where football players are practicing behind the bleachers. The Langley house is the fourth from the right, above the first field light pole. The "new" BGA gym, built in 1948, is in the foreground. The 1906 gym, where Bobby Langley spent hours playing and practicing, is at the other end of the field.

Preface

I've worried and wondered about my mother almost all my life. I worried as a young boy when she and my father were having harsh words and ugly – even physical – disputes. I worried when I saw her challenged by a complicated world that she was not able to understand. I worried when she was alone as my father was being treated at a state hospital for tuberculosis, and I worried when he finally left her a widow.

Ruby Hammox Langley, 1940s

Recently I have realized that a lot of my worry about Ruby Irene Hammox Langley also was worry about myself. When I was growing up I feared that I might have inherited some of her intellectual shortcomings that resulted from her parents being first cousins, shortcomings I could see in the physical handicaps of her brothers and sisters, my aunts and uncles. Because of that, I held myself back from difficult school work and limited my expectations about my future.

Long after her death, I still wonder about her, and how she managed to carry on through her harsh life and intellectual challenges and raise children who, for the most part, overcame their upbringing in shabby conditions with few comforts and limited money. I wonder whether I actually did inherit traits from her – but traits that were good and strong, not bad and limiting. As I reflect on my life, and on the lives of those I know who grew up in similar circumstances, I think that perhaps she passed on strengths that got her through a difficult life that mostly involved things like poverty and domestic violence, a life in which she never drove a car, never owned a home, an didn't even have indoor plumbing until she was 35 years old.

The Depression-era child of itinerant farm workers died in 1998, just as I was getting ready to conclude my own successful business and amid the academic and athletic successes of my children, her grandchildren.

Could she be considered a success in life? Was my success in life despite her, or because of her?

My older brother J.T. earnestly believes that angels were there to help her through a world that she didn't always understand. When I reflect on her life as I saw it, I think he must be right.

Chapter 1: free lunch

Hwy. 31 south from Nashville once was one of the country's main highways, leading from the top of the Michigan mitten to Mobile, Alabama.

The highway passes through the middle of Nashville, then goes south through the hills to Williamson County. As it passes through Franklin, the county seat, the highway becomes Main Street, then splits away diagonally becoming Columbia Avenue, forming an intersection known as Five Points.

Today that intersection is part of Historic Downtown Franklin – a tourism marketing term applied to a lovingly restored area of restaurants and boutiques where locals bring their out of town guests.

In the 1940s it was just "downtown," where people shopped, went to court, visited doctors. The South Central Bell building at Five Points, where operators spoke to you by name as they connected your telephone calls, marked the beginning of West Main Street. Today that building is a yogurt shop. Across the street was the Corner Drugstore, now a Starbucks coffee. The Presbyterian church on the northeast corner now is known as the Historic Presbyterian Church. The 1935 Post Office building survives in the same function today.

On the fifth corner – a wedge between Columbia and West Main – was Franklin Elementary, the only building that is no longer there. That's where my story begins.

In 1948 I was a second grader going to school at Franklin Elementary. I could walk to school in about 20 minutes from my house up the hill in Beasley Town.

There were fine homes on the streets down around the school. There were sidewalks and shade trees

Beasley Town had neither of those. It was built for workers at the Beasley sawmill. Landscaping hadn't been a priority, nor had plumbing. By 1948 the sawmill had been shut down, but the three-room "shotgun" houses were still being rented by poor black and white families for $12 a month. My family was one of them.

The houses were at the edge of Natchez, a neighborhood that had been home to African American Franklin since after the Civil War. On the other side of Beasley Town was Battle Ground Academy, a private school for boarding and local students that had been on the site since 1898.

Second grade was an important year for me. My memories of the school are strong, and I get emotional thinking about that year and how my understanding of my family and my situation changed then. I can remember clearly today how I felt, dealing with what I had to and setting a series of patterns that served me and shaped me as I grew up.

I knew we were poor. I knew that some people looked down on us for where we lived. I knew enough by then to be vague about it when somebody asked me where I lived, but some things were obvious.

Every Monday at school kids had to go up, one at a time, and put their lunch money on the teacher's desk. I never did go up. So everybody in the class knew that I and a few other kids got their lunch free. I was ashamed of that.

My awakening that year was to the fact that I was going to have to deal with things myself that most of my second grade classmates took for granted.

It was a simple thing that awakened me to that reality, and to things about my family that took me years to fully understand.

My teacher, Miss Eulalie Jefferson, announced to my class that they would not be eating lunch at school the next day. Gayle Howard's family had invited everyone to her house for birthday cake and ice cream. The children all should bring a sack lunch.

For most of the children and their parents – even the other poor kids – a sack lunch was a simple request. But I knew right away that this situation was going to be complicated. I had never brought my own lunch to school before.

Most of the kids were excited when school let out. But as I walked up the hill to my house on Granbury Street, I didn't have a good feeling. As usual, my mother was busy with the household chores when I got home. I interrupted her to tell her about the party and about the lunch.

"Ain't no sack lunch," she replied. "You get your lunch free, at school."
I explained again about the birthday party. But my mother raised her voice, as if I hadn't listened the first time. "Ain't got no sack lunch."

And that was it.

We didn't buy sliced bread. We didn't have stuff to fix lunch. We were on welfare. She scolded me real hard not because she was mad at me, but because school parties and sack lunches were beyond her experience. To her I was talking nonsense. She'd never been asked to deal with anything like that, even though to most people it would be a simple request. I knew at that young age that I had found out something about my mother and the type family that I was in. We were different, and poverty was just one of the reasons. This would have a bearing on the rest of my life. I was an 8-year-old kid. I knew I'd have to handle this myself.

Miss Jefferson's Second Grade class, Franklin Elementary, 1948

Gayle Howard was queen of the day the next morning, and there was excitement in the classroom. Sack lunches were piled on a table in Miss Jefferson's room, to be taken by Mrs. Howard and the room mothers to Gayle Howard's house. When the final call came to get all the lunches on the table, I just stayed quiet.

We marched from the school at Five Points to the Howard home on Lewisburg Avenue in just over 15 minutes. They let us play in the large, shady back yard while Mrs. Howard and the room mothers set out the cake, ice cream and sack lunches.

I didn't have to worry about lunch now. I was running around the yard with my friends Ned Sullivan, Billy Speck, Tom Fox and Dennis Bush. When the call came telling us all to come to the lunch table, I made up my mind pretty quick how I was going to handle the situation. I slipped into the bushes at just the right time as all the other kids were running toward the table. I hadn't planned this because I had no idea what to expect at Gayle Howard's house.

But I knew my buddies wouldn't spend a whole lot of time on eating or birthday formalities when there were trees to be climbed and new territory to be explored. And as I watched I knew it was all going to work out. They wolfed down their lunches and their cake, and headed out to the yard again.

And just like that, I was running with them. Even they didn't know that I hadn't been at the lunch table. I still had my self-respect, and I learned a technique that I used again and again as I grew up. I was on my own.

Chapter 2: Stern heritage

My father, Tyree Eugene Langley, grew up on the same farm as his namesake and grandfather, Tyree Lafayette Holland. As the firstborn, he would have been an heir to the gently rolling land south of Franklin along Duplex Road near Spring Hill that came into the Holland family as a federal land grant for service in the Revolutionary War.

My grandfather, Albert Eugene Langley, had been grooming Tyree to take over the farm his entire life with hard work and discipline, and respect for his family name. He was a stern and serious man. His was a life of here and now, chores to be done, taking care of business; not of stories, not of family history.

I knew that my father's name came from my great grandfather, Tyree Lafayette Holland. But I didn't learn until I was 45 years old that Holland was a Confederate soldier who in 1862 joined Nathan Bedford Forrest's famously effective cavalry unit. After seeing action in Atlanta, Chattanooga and Chickamauga, Tyree Holland was captured in 1864 in retreat near Calhoun, Georgia. He went with a trainload of prisoners to Nashville then Louisville, where – at that late stage in the war – prisoners were given the option of switching sides if they swore an oath of allegiance to the United States. Tyree Holland would not accept the oath, and ended up a prisoner at Rock Island Barracks, Illinois, for almost a year before the war ended in 1865. At the end of the war he was released, and he walked more than 600 miles home.

Tyree Lafayette Holland

Great Grandfather Holland dedicated himself to the dairy and tobacco farm and didn't marry until 17 years after his return from prison. He was 39, and his bride, "Mattie" Glenn, was 22 and from a nearby farm in a community called Duplex. She bore him a daughter, Sophia, in 1885, and another, Cynthia Clair, in 1887.

Albert Eugene (Papa Gene) Langley and Cynthia Clair Holland Langley, 1920s.

At age 43, Tyree Holland passed away a few months after Cynthia Clair was born.

Cynthia Clair's marriage to Albert Eugene Langley – another descendant of early Middle Tennessee settlers – brought the Langley name to the farm.

But Cynthia Clair died in January, 1925, when her son, Tyree Eugene Langley, was 15. That greatly affected the boy, who was very close to his mother, with whom he shared the special bond of a firstborn. His mother was his protector and most likely would have pushed him to finish school, and perhaps reined in the wild ways and drinking that he fell into later.

Tyree Eugene chafed under the discipline of his grieving father. Without his mother to intervene on his behalf, or to urge him to continue his schooling, he got involved with another restless teenager from the next farm over. She became pregnant and bore a son, William. Their marriage met the fate of so many teenage marriages as Tyree remained restless and rebellious, and unwilling to settle into the role of a young parent.

He left his young bride and began building a reputation as a drinker, a skirt chaser, and a street runner. He had a big personality and became friends with moonshiners, and developed into a charismatic fixture at parties who could dance and teach others to dance. He discovered the honky tonk life and developed a lifelong taste for alcohol.

Papa Gene Langley, center, poses with the children of Cynthia Holland Langley, from left, Tyree Langley, Polly Langley, William ("Mum") Langley, Hilliard Lee Langley, and Perry Langley.

His behavior did not go over well with my grandfather, who still had to face the family of the girl he had left with a child.

Yet despite his wild streak, Tyree Langley also built a reputation as a solid worker and he ended up finding work on the farms of my grandfather's peers for the next 10 years while living the night life of a restless young man. He had an eye for pretty girls and a talent for reeling them in.

Chapter 3: Teen-age bride

In 1934, Tyree Langley was working as a foreman, or straw boss, on the Rufus Ogilvie farm, just a few miles up Buckner Lane from the Langley-Holland place. With cattle, sheep, grain, row crops, and tobacco, the farm needed a workforce. One day Mr. Ogilvie told him that a new tenant farm family was expected.

Depression-era tenant farmers lived in small houses on the farms, and the living quarters were considered part of their meager pay. Tenant farmers were farm workers, not sharecroppers. They were commonly known as "white trash" or even "white slaves" because they never could accumulate property or possessions, like cars.

But the Hammox family arrived in a Model T.

Though John Wesley Hammox was illiterate, he was known as a "fix-it" guy, who was good with cars and farm machinery. That talent was his foot in the door. Tyree Langley was watching when the family drove up the dusty road to the Ogilvie farm.

Five children piled out of the car along with John Hammox and his wife, Pinky Belle. Three of the children were visibly handicapped. But what caught Tyree Langley's eye was the oldest daughter, Ruby Irene, who at 15 was approaching the height of her beauty.

My father was 26 at the time.

His attention to the young girl did not escape the notice of the girl's mother – my grandmother – Pinky Belle Hammox. From that first day, when she noticed him eyeing Ruby, she never trusted my dad. It wasn't too long before she felt like she knew his ways, and warned her daughter about him and young men like him.

My mother, Ruby Irene, picked up on Tyree's interest, too. But rather than be wary of him like her mother was, the teenage girl

John Hammox and Pinky Belle Fitts Hammox

was attracted by his charms. A man's attention to her as a young woman was something new in her life, which so far had been as a child in isolated, primitive tenant houses.

As the Hammox family settled in to the tenant house on the Ogilvie farm and Ruby got to know Tyree Langley. She found out that he had been married, and that he had a son. He had come from a rooted, landed family and lived in a world that she hadn't seen. I think she fell in love with him.

Tyree began opening up that world to her. He took her to picnics and parties. She was too young for the honky tonks, but he had friends who would throw parties where someone might pull out a fiddle and another would bring a banjo. They would move the furniture out of the living room and dance all night. Tyree taught Ruby how to dance at those parties.

As he courted Ruby Irene and worked with the Hammoxes on the farm, he began to learn about her family.

John Hammox and Pinky Belle Fitts were first cousins. Years before, they had traveled to Nashville to find work. They got jobs at Werthan Bag, a factory for burlap and cotton bags. Not long after, they married.

After Ruby was born in 1920, they left the city and John Hammox found work back on the livestock farms in the rolling green hills of Williamson County.

Their family began to grow. The couple's status as first cousins greatly affected their children. Vester, who was troubled all her life with obesity, was their second daughter. John Wesley Hammox Jr., known as Bug, could not speak clearly. Dorothy, their fourth child, had to use braces on her legs to walk, and had gnarled hands. The baby, James, spoke clearly but also had drawn up hands and deformed legs.

None of this discouraged Tyree Langley in his pursuit of young Ruby, who listened to the warnings of her mother and never gave in to his sexual advances.

But a year and a half later – on Aug. 20, 1936, they got married. My father moved in to the crowded tenant house with the Hammox family.

Tyree was in for an awakening of his own. He had lived a free life since

Ruby Hammox Langley and Tyree Eugene Langley on their wedding day

his teenage marriage, and suddenly he was a married man again.

Even though he was the foreman at the farm and had dealt with tenants before, I'm not so sure whether he was ever sober enough to realize what he was going to get into if he married this young girl.

First, there were the issues of her background, and the physical problems plaguing her siblings. Second, his family would not accept this poor, inbred tenant farmer family.

Chapter 4: Pregnant, intimidated

Things had changed during Tyree's absence at the Langley-Holland place on Duplex Road.

Lela Gardner Langley poses with Papa Gene Langley on their wedding day

His widower father Albert Eugene Langley had remarried a young school teacher, Lela Gardner, in 1926. She had come to the area from the Water Valley community in Maury County to teach school. In 1929 they started a family of their own, and ended up bringing six more children into the world.

Despite the new Langley children, there was still more space at the farm for my father and his wife than in the Hammox tenant house. Tyree and Ruby moved to the Langley-Holland place.

Young Ruby, now 16, began calling my grandfather Papa Gene, and his wife Mama Lela.

Mama Lela took her under wing and began educating her about housekeeping, cooking and the duties of a farm wife. My mother was always grateful to Mama Lela for her kindness. But Papa Gene was stern and serious. He never did accept Ruby Irene, and my mother always sensed that. Her own father, Papa John, was a hardworking man, but he was easygoing and kind with his children. At the Langley place, she was around a whole lot of people who were intimidating to her.

Papa Gene – as before – was hard on my father, another thing that made my mother feel that she wasn't wanted there. Now pregnant, my mother began to urge my father to get the two of them off the family farm.

It was about that time that Tyree landed a good job that gave them the income they needed to move out on their own. He became a driver for Brittain and Fristoe Purina Feed Store in Franklin, which had contracts with many of the dairy farmers in southern Williamson County to pick up heavy cans of fresh milk seven days a week.

From front, Bobby, J.T. and Hubert Lee pose with their mother in front of their father's milk truck about 1942.

He was on the road at dawn, summer or winter, rain or shine. But he was finished by mid-day. The job was a hard one, but the pay was good for the times.

Ruby gave birth to Hubert Lee shortly before she and Tyree moved to a house in Spring Hill, then a few urban style blocks surrounded by rural countryside. There they rented rooms and shared space with two other families.

Even though he had to make the milk run seven days a week, my father felt free again being out on the road, away from the demands of Papa Gene. His time off in the afternoons and late evenings also gave him a chance to go back to his old ways: drinking and dancing at the roadhouses.

His partner in drinking – and his co-worker on the milk truck, was a man named Reuben "Duck" McLemore. After a few years of working and drinking together, my father and Duck McLemore were like brothers. From the time I was born, Duck McLemore was a fixture in our family, and was the first black person that any of my siblings ever knew. I remember him as friendly, fun and nice, playing with us, letting us climb up on the milk truck. We were always excited to see him. My father's closeness to him influenced all of us, and our subsequent attitudes toward race. My mother also was very fond of Duck.

My mother had been happy to get away from the Langley farm. But now she was often alone with a young baby, and it wasn't long before she was pregnant again, this time with my brother John Tyree, known as J.T. and named for Papa John.

Ruby Irene started complaining about my father coming home late, often with alcohol on his breath. My father didn't always respond well to that.

By now the Hammox family had left the Ogilvie farm and were tenants at Warioto Farm, owned by the Werthans, the same family that owned the Nashville factory where John and Pinky Belle Hammox had worked before they were married. Warioto Farm was a prosperous and beautiful place with white fences and green-roofed barns and fields of livestock feed crops. The farm was in the business of breeding, raising and training three- and five-gaited show horses. And like his talent for machinery, my grandfather Papa John Hammox also had a gift for horses.

Papa John regularly visited my mother in Spring Hill, and knew that my father left her alone a lot. I suppose she must have talked to Papa John about my dad's drinking and carousing, because one day Ruby left the Spring Hill house with Papa John and went home with him to the Werthan place, where the family now lived in a tenant house far out in the fields without electricity or running water.

It wasn't long before my father showed up in the milk truck and talked her into coming back to the two rooms in the Spring Hill boarding house, now with two babies, my brothers. And she left him a couple more times after the same arguments about his honky tonk life style, his lack of help with the two babies, and his spending.

In late 1939 Ruby became pregnant again, this time with me. I was born June 6, 1940. Both my father and my mother knew that now, with three young boys, the boarding house wouldn't do.

My father spotted a shabby old house for rent near the beginning of his milk route on Lewisburg Pike in the Duplex community, where my great grandmother had come from. Part of the house had rotted floors and couldn't be used. But the rooms that were left gave us more space than the boarding house.

Chapter 5: Stolen coal

My memories as a young child begin in the Lewisburg Pike house. I remember good things, good feelings and togetherness as a family. I also remember being afraid, not understanding, and being sad sometimes for my mother.

Everybody slept in one room with a coal stove. There was a wood stove in the back room where my mother cooked.

Tyree Langley would get paid every week on Friday afternoon. Many times he wouldn't come home until Saturday morning, and he wouldn't have any money left from his pay.

On cold winter nights when my father wouldn't come home, we sometimes ran out of coal. My mother would just put us to bed so we could stay warm. Sometimes we were scared, especially when our father yelled at our mother. Sometimes we felt isolated and lonely.

Sometimes my father would steal coal from Mount Carmel Church across the road, or from a schoolhouse that wasn't too far.

We didn't have a lot of other families to compare ourselves to, except those of my mother and my father. But we knew that our daddy wasn't exactly treating my mother and the rest of us the way he should be. I remember times when my mother would go off by herself and cry. I remember trying to comfort her with hugs and pats and affection.

Once in a while Papa Gene would visit us. My mother said later that she remembered Papa Gene taking my father outside and lecturing him about the sorry state of our family.

Despite my father's behavior, he was our dad and we all knew that he loved us, even though he wasn't a good provider.

There weren't any neighbors close by, and no other kids to play with. We didn't go places other than occasional family visits. My dad would load up the kids and Ruby Irene on the milk truck sometimes and we would go off to visit Papa John.

Tyree would start drinking when we got there, and still be drinking when we left. My mother would be mad at him. With whiskey on his breath, he'd playfully pick up the kids, toss us into the air. He would always make everyone laugh … except when he would have too much to drink and become a little bit abusive with his discipline. I remember the smell of his breath and the look in his eye from those times. Later I used those signals as my warning to get away.

Ruby holds baby Mary Clair at the dilapidated house in the Duplex community.

He also sometimes would take all of the kids to Papa Gene's: a totally different experience because Papa Gene was a pretty stern guy, disappointed by the lot of his oldest son. The Langley boys would drink together, but Papa Gene never touched a drop. Ruby Irene spent a lot of those days at the Langley place alone or with us. She couldn't relax much there because she still felt that the Langleys looked down on her.

When World War II came along, my parents had three kids, and one on the way. Because of the children and because of his job, my father was exempt from the draft. As a dairy driver he was considered an essential worker because he helped supply fresh milk to the troops at Camp Forrest and Fort Campbell.

In 1942 Mary Clair Langley was born at the Lewisburg Pike house. She was named for our grandmother, Cynthia Clair Holland Langley, the daughter of the Civil War soldier. And like my father's bond with his mother, he had a special bond with his first born daughter. He protected her all his life, and she never acknowledged his faults as the rest of us did.

Chapter 6: Whiskey and tuberculosis

The Great Depression officially was over when World War II started, but many parts of the South, including rural Middle Tennessee, hadn't quite recovered. Yet amid the widespread rural poverty – or maybe because of it – there was community and people helped their neighbors.

Clint Thompson and his family were among those who helped my family. He owned Thompson's Store. All of his children lived around him. In addition to the store, they farmed. They didn't have tractors, but still plowed and planted with mule power. My dad and Duck McLemore picked up their milk, and gave them very good service.

The Thompsons knew my father's faults, and sometimes brought us food from their farm. After Mary Clair was born they let us move into one of their tenant

Barefoot Bobby, Hubert Lee and J.T. take time out from playing to pose.

houses a little closer to Franklin. They let my dad and the family live there free, probably because they knew he wouldn't pay them regularly anyway.

Like the other house, this one had no electricity. We didn't even have a well: we got our water out of a spring. We had no radio. But my dad brought home newspapers after his milk runs, and my mother taught herself to read with them. With a war going on, the papers were our only source of news.

In early summer we'd go blackberry picking, My mother would get coal oil and tie rags soaked with it around our legs to keep the chiggers off of us as we moved through the tall grass around the berry canes, but we got 'em anyway.

My mother cherished her children. She played with us and took care of us, and if we needed an ass-whipping, she would give us one. We were together and there were good feelings and memories of that, but we were lonely a lot.

My mother didn't know any other kind of life. She was born into a family that worked hard but stayed poor. And she married into a similar situation. She was married to a man that she loved. She also admired him because to her he seemed to be at ease in a world that intimidated her. She knew all of his faults, and suffered from them. But she stayed with him. Where else would she go?

During our stay on the Thompson farm, my awareness grew of things about my family. I remember noticing that my father was changing. His drinking and not coming home had been balanced by his strong personality and his status among his brothers, and even at the Hammox house, as the life of the party. The drinking and not coming home continued, but the happy go lucky times were fewer and fewer. He was becoming harder to live with.

Frequently, his behavior scared us and made us fear for our mother. He would get mad. I can remember his voice shouting "stupid" and "bitch" at my mother, and saying insulting things about her family. There were occasions where he slapped her or hit her with his fists and blacked her eyes and knocked her to the floor. We were too small to stand up to him, and we knew it. We stayed out of the way, but as soon as he left we would try to comfort her.

He was frustrated by conditions that he created himself, including the fact that he was married to a young woman who frequently didn't know what he was talking about. His frustrations were taken out on my mother and taken out on us too. We were isolated and didn't have a lot of exposure to how other families lived, but we knew that his drinking, his temper and his violence weren't right.

We also began to notice our dad's coughing, and losing weight. He was quick to anger, and he didn't want us around making noise. Though alcohol seemed to have had power over him for many years, it seemed that now something else was wrong. His cough just kept getting worse.

I don't know how he ended up going to the doctor, but when he finally went, he didn't come back. Tyree Langley had tuberculosis. The doctors said they hadn't seen anybody that with a case of TB as bad as his.

Ruby Irene Langley now was 25 years old and pregnant with her fifth child. I was five years old. She was worried that my father might not ever come home again. As scared as we were when he was on one of his rampages, we were more scared now.

Chapter 7: Chased out of a dream

The highest time of my early childhood, and the lowest, came on the same day.

It also was the day that indelibly enshrined Papa John Hammox as one of the greatest people my brothers and sisters have ever known – a man of kindness and devotion to the family.

With our father in a state tuberculosis hospital on the north side of Nashville, it was Papa John who came to the rescue. One day he showed up in his old A-Model Ford and told us that he had found a place for us to live close to where he still was working, at Warioto Farm. He had asked a neighboring farm family if his daughter and her four children could use a vacant tenant house on their property. He was proud to have found us a nicer place.

He borrowed a truck from the Werthan farm, and told my other grandfather, Papa Gene, about the move. Papa Gene showed up to help along with my Uncle Perry.

With all the men there, it didn't take much to pack us up, and it didn't take much of a truck to move what we had.

Papa John had told us all about this house, that it had four rooms and a screened-in back porch. The children were excited as they loaded up in the truck. We all knew that our mother was glad that we were going to be moving closer to her parents, and all of us also looked forward to singing and playing with our aunts, uncles and grandparents, who even had a radio.

We drove down West Harpeth Road in the truck, then crossed the river of the same name. Papa John started pointing to this little tenant house and our excitement grew. We could tell right off the bat that it was nicer than we'd ever imagined.

The yard looked nice. There was a fence around the place and green shutters. Even though I was only five, I remember all this very well, and how happy I was. We jumped out of the truck as fast as we could and ran inside.

The grownups were unloading stuff and we were helping carry things inside when someone looked toward "the big house," where the owner of the farm lived. A dust cloud was being kicked up by a pickup truck coming down the road very fast. The pickup pulled up in front of the tenant house. The door flew open and a man with rage on his reddened face jumped out and walked toward my grandfathers and my uncle.

"Is there someone in this family that's got TB? Is there someone in this family that's got TB?" he shouted twice.

Papa John said quietly that his daughter's husband had TB, but he wouldn't be living there.

The man cursed, and then said, "I'm giving you 30 minutes to get the hell off of my property, and unload that house and get out of here. We're not renting anything to anybody that's got TB."

As long as I live, I can never forget the look on my Papa John's face. And I'll never forget how I felt for my mother. It was one of the saddest times in her life, and the saddest times for us kids.

There was a shocked quiet after the man sped away. My Papa John was the first to break the silence.

"That's OK, they can go with me," he said.

Papa Gene didn't say very much. Though Papa John's face was flushed with anger and embarrassment, Papa Gene didn't seem to be upset at all. He and my Uncle Perry just got in their car and left.

We all climbed back aboard the truck and headed to the Hammox's tenant house on the back side of Joe Werthan's farm, where we were welcomed by my Grandma Pinky Belle, Aunt Vester, Uncle Bug, Aunt Dorothy and Uncle James.

Not long after we moved in, my mother gave birth to her fifth child, Carolyn Ann Langley, a fragile little girl who may have been so because of what my mother had been through during her pregnancy.

Chapter 8: New homes for the boys

Papa John had a big load to carry. He didn't make much working at the farm. Tenant farmers more or less worked for a place to live, and not much of a place, at that. This shabby house had no shade around it. No power. No toilet. These old houses always had a stench about them from people using bedpans when it was too cold to go to the outhouse.

I don't know what happened – maybe Papa Gene was feeling guilty seeing us crowded in that dirty little tenant house. But after Carolyn Ann was born it was agreed that the three boys would go live with Papa Gene and the uncles until we found out what was going to happen with my father. And so it was that the boys left the Werthan farm.

Papa John and Mama had been telling us for a while that Papa Gene would be coming to take us away. Lacking a telephone, we weren't exactly sure when it would happen.

One day we were playing in front of the house, which was on the back of the farm with several fenced pastures between the house and the main road. We heard a car drive up and stop to open the third and final gate on the way to the house. It was Papa Gene and Uncle Perry.

We called out to mama, and she began hurrying around to gather up the few things we had to take with us. Her face was flushed.

It was not a happy occasion for anyone, and Papa Gene and Uncle Perry did not stay long.

I'll never forget when we drove away looking back and seeing my mother crying. I was crying, too. I was scared and disoriented, and had no idea what to expect.

Hubert Lee went to live with Papa Gene Langley. They already were at odds – Hubert Lee had picked up some of my father's defiant ways and Papa Gene still was a disciplinarian. Hubert Lee had to work on the farm with Mama Lela's kids, and sometimes was rebellious.

JT went with my Uncle Perry, Aunt Louise, and their two daughters, Vivian and Linda. They lived on Depot Street in Spring Hill. Uncle Perry was a good man, but always seemed a little cold to us. JT's time with Uncle Perry was not as pleasant as mine, with William Merrill Langley, known to us as Uncle Mum, Aunt Margaret, and their two daughters, Patsy and Marie.

Aunt Margaret was the first lady that I ever came to know closely other than my mother. She and I talked a lot, and she read to me. I felt like there was a bond between us.

Uncle Mum also took a liking to me and he made things good for me. I was a freckle faced boy about the same age as Patsy and Marie, 5 and 6 years old.
Still, for me It was a strange situation. I was scared and wet the bed at night. Aunt Margaret talked to me about that, but she didn't scold me. I loved her, but she wasn't my mother.

Uncle Mum and Aunt Margaret lived only about three blocks from Uncle Perry and Aunt Louise. Sometimes J.T. would slip away from the house and come to see me. He would always get scolded for doing that.

But the excitement of seeing J.T. on those unauthorized visits reminded me of how much I loved and missed my brothers and sisters.

We spent about a year away from my mother. We missed her, but I can only imagine how hard it was for her to be without her three sons. Her children were all she had in her very limited world.

Knowing my mother's situation, and knowing that my dad might not make it, Uncle Mum approached my grandfather once to ask if he could keep me. When my mother got wind of that, she started on a mission to get us back together.

Both the state Health Department and the Welfare Department were involved both in my father's case and in the plight of my mother, who had no education, no job, and five children.

From time to time Papa John would get word from the Health Department about my dad. Sometimes he would take his old Model A Ford to the hospital so my mother could visit him.

My mother couldn't conduct business or talk to people, and in that way wasn't what most people would consider "normal." Despite her intellectual limitations she had been growing a strong will over the years, and with the help of Papa John she began to tell people that she wanted her boys back.

Around the same time, the people at the Health Department were saying that my father could be able to come home soon, but he would need fresh air, and they didn't want him to be that close to other people.

Through the Welfare Department, my mother found out there was an old one-room schoolhouse on in a wooded area on Hillsboro Road going north out of Franklin toward Nashville, about 15 miles north of us. It was surrounded by farms and rural property. Its isolation would be perfect for a TB patient. Working with health and welfare officials and the Williamson County school board, she and Papa John got it worked out in 1946 that Ruby Langley and her five children could move into the old Parman School.

We were in for a happy time, back together as a family.

After we had lived a year away from our mother and sisters, Papa John showed up at our uncle's houses in Spring Hill to pick up J.T., Hubert Lee and me to take us to the schoolhouse.

My mother was already there waiting for us with the two little girls: Mary Clair, 4 and Carolyn, about a year old.

Chapter 9: School in the woods

The idea of living in a schoolhouse was exciting. It was fun to live in one big room. The school furniture was still there. There was an old blackboard and a stage. There were woods all around, and fields.

Tyree, just home from the hospital, hugs little Carolyn while surrounded by his children, Mary Clair, Hubert Lee, J.T. and Bobby outside the old Parman School north of Franklin.

The most fun was the fact that we were all back together. After spending a year in different homes, we three boys were excited and delighted with our new circumstances.

But I still could see the stress in my mother's face as she waited for my father to show up. She knew he had been seriously ill and wasn't sure what to expect in his needs or his temperament.

We got word that they had done surgery on him and he could go home soon. After a few days, Papa Gene and Uncle Perry brought Tyree Langley to the old school.

Though my mother had visited him during his hospitalization, the children hadn't, and when I first saw him he didn't look like the same person. He got out of the car and still had his pajamas on. He had lost a lot of his hair and looked almost like he had been in a concentration camp. He was moving slowly. He would never be the same man again. He coughed all the time, but he still smoked Lucky Strikes. He had to spit into jars that the Health Department would come and pick up for testing. This was one of the few times there was no alcohol in his life, but it wouldn't be long before that would come back. After Papa Gene and Uncle Perry brought my father to the schoolhouse, we didn't see them again for a while. There was a fear of TB at that time and they didn't want to be around us. As a child I wondered about why they didn't come around, and as an adult I have wondered many times how Papa Gene would have reacted if another one of his sons – one with fewer faults and a less controversial marriage than my father – had come down with tuberculosis. I kind of feel like he left us out to graze, and left it to the welfare department and the churches to look after us.

We did see Papa John, however. He regularly showed up and took us to town. Some of the Fitts family, my grandmother's people, also would come and visit us.

As a "TB family," we also got visits from the Health Department. The nurses would come and talk to my mother and tell her that everything had to be clean, sheets, dishes, my father, the floors. My mother took every word to heart, and did everything they told her to do, spending her days scrubbing the schoolhouse floors, washing dishes, and doing laundry. Sometimes the nurses would come get us and take us into town for skin tests and X-rays.

At the time, Williamson County had one of the highest TB rates in the United States, but nobody knew why. Some people blamed milk, or cattle, and Williamson County was one of the top dairy counties in the state. Unpasteurized milk was thought to be one way the disease was transmitted. My father's job involved working with unpasteurized milk every day, so that may have been how he was infected.

Still, I think that his drinking and carousing probably made him vulnerable to the infection. I think that he brought this on himself. Now 38 years old, he would be sick the rest of his days.

My memories of living in the old Parman school mostly are good ones, in large part because I was so happy to be with my reunited family. We had to get used to my dad again, and ended up spending most of our time outside, because my dad didn't want anybody to make any noise. Most days being outside was no problem for three active boys – me 6, J.T. 7½, and Hubert Lee, 9. We ran and played in the woods. We climbed trees and played Army and got sprayed by skunks and got into other mischief. As soon as it got warm, we never wore shoes.

The isolated, forested area was not a problem for my mother, either. She had an outdoors side. Her father, Papa John, had always been a hunter and a trapper, and was a good shot with a rifle or a shotgun. My mother, then 26, also knew how to shoot. I remember one day she stepped out of the schoolhouse and shot two foxes with a .22 rifle that Papa John had given her.

So, the Health Department's intention to keep us isolated in the school was a success. I think the word had spread around that there was a family that lived there that the dad had tuberculosis, so most people steered clear.

I remember only one visit from a neighbor: a lady that stopped by to see my mother. She lived on the Pewitt Farm on Berrys Chapel Road, just north of the old school. She told my mother that if she would send the boys over to the farm, she would give us some milk. Given our isolated life, the kindness of this stranger was a big deal for us and a it remains a significant memory of that time.

For my mother, life got back on track at the old schoolhouse. The family was back together and she didn't have to worry about where our dad was – whether he was out at some beer joint or honky tonk.

But late in 1946 my dad had to go back to the hospital. Before he left he looked for a place in town for the family to live. He was concerned about my mother being out that far in the country, alone with the children in this old school.

Grandma Pinky Belle had two brothers, Charlie Fitts and Richard Fitts who lived in Franklin in a place informally called Beasley Town. My father had asked my great uncles to let him know if one of the Beasley Town houses came open, and eventually one of them passed the word that one had.

My father left for the hospital, and one more time, Papa John came with the truck and again we were on our way to a new place and a new life. Ruby Langley and her five children were coming to Beasley Town in Franklin.

Chapter 10: Living around people

All the small towns that surrounded Nashville in the mid-1940s still had sections with no electricity, no running water, and outhouses. Beasley Town was one of them.

It was a low-rent place for poor people, black and white – people even too poor to live in their respective segregated neighborhoods of the time. In a way we were socially advanced in learning to live in our own integrated society before its time came in the larger community. We also learned that the way we lived was very different from people who lived just one or two blocks away. Beasley Town had no plumbing. People used outhouses and got their water from two wells. The well for all the people on our end of Beasley Town was right by our house, and all the residents walked down there to draw their water out.

For my mother, who always had lived in the country, having neighbors and activity around took some adjustment. But having her uncles nearby helped, and she got used to it. It probably was the first time in my mother's life that she felt safe and secure living around other people.

Living in Franklin was an eye opener for us kids, too, after being isolated so much of our early lives. We learned a lot about people, and about generosity and friendliness, prejudice and snobbery.

It seems like everything we needed there cost $12: rent, a load of coal, or a load of wood. The three-room houses were identical, and were close together.

It was up to my mother to make it work out, and she did, with the help of the state. And though many people in town looked down on families that got welfare, she considered it just a thing that had to be.

Franklin at the time had a population of about 6,000 people, and those people would talk. Word got around about good deeds, misdeeds and special needs. Someone at the Fourth Avenue Church of Christ – then the biggest church in town – heard from the Welfare Department about the woman in Beasley Town with the five children and the husband in the hospital. A group from the church visited my mother and invited her to bring the family to church.

On Sunday a church bus driven by Mr. Buford Blackman lumbered up the street and we got on board. In a sense, my mother stayed aboard: She remained loyal to that church the rest of her life.

For my siblings and I, going to church was intimidating. Even as a seven-year-old kid I knew I didn't have nice clothes on like the other kids. To us, it was embarrassing that some people we met in Sunday School would come by our house and give us clothes that they were going to get rid of. I don't think my mother ever thought a thing about it. She didn't see the world the way we did.

But it began to open our eyes to the fact that Beasley Town was at the edge of a world that was totally different, surrounded as it was by nice neighborhoods and comfortable families. We had been sad, and scared, and sometimes uncomfortable in our lives, but for the first time we developing a sense of shame about being poor and living the way we did.

When we first moved to Beasley Town, my mother was protective of us and made us stay close to home. As she grew comfortable with the place, she let us drift away down the street to play and make friends. Some of those childhood friends are still my friends today.

Across from our house was Battle Ground Academy, a private school for local and boarding students. There was a football field on campus and two or three practice fields. We didn't know anything about sports at the time, but we always knew that we could run. And when we joined the integrated group of Beasley Town kids in pickup football games on those fields, we found out how fast we were.

Our gang included Robert Junior Williams and Early Ellison, who were about my age, and Goldie Dixon and Jesse Turner, who were about Hubert Lee's age. All four were black, so they went to different schools and couldn't always go to places that we could. Then there was Wayne Beard, whom we later nicknamed "Buck," and whose mother always bragged about being a Cherokee Indian. And of course there was my tomboy sister, Mary Clair, who was welcome in all of the games once everyone learned how fast she was.

Buck Beard was a skinny little kid who used words like I had never heard, like he invented cussing. He couldn't say anything without cussing. He also would fight anybody, even his friends, including me.

Wayne "Buck" Beard, 1948

I'd play cowboys and Indians with Buck Beard. We would build forts, and in doing so I started to learn about the Battle of Franklin, and the fact that Beasley Town was built on one of the hottest of the Civil War battle's hot spots. We would be digging out a fort and come up with bullets and belt buckles and other relics from the war. Those items are prized now but were just part of the landscape then. Battle Ground Academy was named because of what happened there in 1864, but at that time there wasn't much nostalgia about that unpleasant event in Franklin history. Still, I remember thinking about the young soldiers that were killed in my front yard and my back yard, and all over BGA. Some old people talked about the Battle of Franklin, but we never heard about it in school.

We had our own world when we played together. We all knew that we all lived in Beasley Town and we all knew that everybody who lived there was poor. I don't deny that I was ashamed of where we lived, but I was always proud of the friends that I had there.

We'd gone to school on and off during our recent life on the move, but it had all been so disorganized that we all started over. I started first grade at Franklin Elementary School a year older than the rest of the kids.

About the time school was going to start, my father came back

Aunt Dorothy Hammox made this photo of Ruby, Tyree and Carolyn Langley in Beasley Town. Tyree is still wearing his pajamas from the hospital.

from the hospital for the second time. By then he'd had three or four surgeries, but I'm not sure he was any better. His case was one that he was never going to get over easily.

He had good days and bad days, but most of his days were bad days. His temper was short. He was not able to work. He always looked so bad, and for the rest of his life he never quit coughing. We just finally had to get used to it, mostly by trying to stay out of the house when we could.

He would never admit that he had brought it on himself, and continued to do things that weren't good for his health. Occasionally he would find a way to run into some of his old buddies. They knew he wasn't doing very well, and that's probably why they would often favor him with a drink.

When he felt good enough he would get out and make the rounds of places and friends or hang around the cab stand off the Franklin town square. It was very obvious that he'd started drinking again. My mother could always smell it on him, and we could, too. Where he got the money, I don't know. He had no income at all. The only income we had was welfare. But he seemed to always know how to get it, and drink it, and it always changed his personality.

It also changed the mood of the household. He and my mother always had some harsh words and we had to deal with that. And again he was calling our mother names, like he had years ago.

Every so often the Health Department people would come and take him for a checkup, to make sure he hadn't had a relapse and wasn't going to spread TB to us. I wonder how many discussions the medical people had with him about how he didn't seem to be trying to do any better to get well, to get his body back to where he could get on with a good life. Doctors always know when people drink and I'm sure it was obvious with my father.

All of us understood the situation, and we were determined to move forward and be happy.

He disappointed us a lot, and frightened us regularly, but later in life I learned to appreciate a lot of the discipline he passed on to us, and how he taught us how to be courteous to people, how to open doors for ladies, how to say yes sir and no ma'am. He taught us table manners, things that our mother couldn't teach us. He taught us to be on time, and to work hard. As life goes on you can learn to forgive your parents for their human failings.

He was my dad, and I carried the memories of when we were younger and he was a happier man who usually was the life of the party. For a long time I had hope that he would get better and I believed there was a possibility that he would quit drinking and straighten his life out.

During the next few years Beasley Town really became our home. We didn't invite any school friends home, and none came by, but we grew closer to the families that lived around us.

Summer nights were pleasant. I remember black and white boys from Beasley town going down to Porky's Store to get an RC Cola and a Popsicle. I remember black and white neighbors in Beasley town playing cards together outside.

Years later I still remember the smell of the place: wood smoke and coal smoke and frying potatoes. I remember coal soot boiling out of the chimneys on Granbury, Natchez and Carter streets. People would let the coal fires burn down during the daytime, then stoke the stoves for the evening chill. I remember my mother and other women going out to get their laundry in before the soot started falling, and ruining a whole day's work.

My brothers and I never talked about how our mother was, but I certainly thought about it and I suppose they did too. We had seen our aunts and uncles crippled, and we were getting to the age that we were beginning to figure out that what afflicted them also afflicted her, in a different way. When I finally was old enough to understand what made my mother different from other mothers, and how that related to her brothers and sisters, it changed my whole life and implanted a fear of what she may have passed on to us.

We'd also just about figured out the situation we were in with our dad. I was 8, then 9, then 10 years old before I finally accepted the fact that he wasn't going to stop drinking and his health wasn't going to get much better.

Eventually, though, my father felt good enough that he could go work at the cab stand for Mr. J.E. Ragan, who had Ragan Cab Company right off the Franklin Square. Mr. Ragan once had been a milk man like my father. They were old drinking buddies from way back.

My dad would go down to the cab stand and answer the telephone. He knew the county very well and was sort of a dispatcher. He made enough money to keep him in his booze.

We didn't mind that his job didn't help the family much financially. It was just good to get him out of the house.

Chapter 11: Life on the sidelines

Throughout my growing up there were special people who influenced me or helped my family in a special way. J.B. Akin was one of them.

He was the coach at Battle Ground Academy, where I was introduced to sports by watching the BGA students play. When they weren't playing, Mr. Akin let the Beasley Town kids use the fields and gyms – even the black kids, who were not allowed to use the public fields at the County Center unless it was closed.

The County Center was just a short distance through the brush on the other side of our house. It included a rodeo arena, athletic fields for Franklin High School, tennis and basketball courts. It was ironic that the black kids couldn't use it because the County Center was surrounded on two sides by black neighborhoods, and the racially mixed Beasley Town on the third side. The black kids were our friends and playmates, and we knew that it was wrong that we could play there and they couldn't, but they accepted it and we accepted it, and we just moved on.

As 5-, 6-, 7-, and 8-year-old kids, we picked up the sports quickly. We saw sports going on around us all the time, and the coaches, staff and students were good to us. We would even participate when they would let us. Coach Akin was kind to us. He learned our names, and let us hang around during practice.

One day the Beasley Town kids were watching as the BGA football team was running drills on the practice field. We were always around, shagging balls for the team.

For one drill, they had all taken their helmets off. Somehow, my little sister Carolyn had left our house and snuck across the street. We didn't even notice she was there until we saw her sitting, pants down, on one of the helmets. It must have looked like a bedpan turned up for her, and she used it. We all took off running. It wasn't long after that that they put a big fence around the playing field, though I don't really think the helmet incident was the reason.

In addition to the fence, BGA built a new gym, which provided lots of excitement and entertainment for all the kids from Beasley Town as it went up. From the day they laid the foundation, my brother Hubert Lee was determined that he was going to be the first one to shoot a goal in that new gym. It was finished in 1948.

One day the workers brought the goals in. We saw them lying on the floor, and found out that the crews were going to put them up the next day.

We ran home from school the next day, and then ran across the street to the old gym to get a ball. And when we went into the new gym, the goals had been installed. There was no net up yet, but Hubert Lee shot the first goal and always was real proud of that.

Without radio, or TV, or magazines, or newspapers, my sports heroes were the 1948-49 class at Battle Ground Academy, hall of famers like Gerald Johnson, Ralph Brown, Tommy Robinson, James Lofton, Tyler Berry, and Billy Isaacs, and Franklin High stars like J.B. Chester, David Johnston, and Bobby T. Ladd. The athletes were our role models, and we admired the ones that displayed both talent and good sportsmanship.

The morning after a Friday night football game the Beasley Town kids would get up early to crawl under the grandstands and look for change. If you could go under there and find a quarter, you had hit the jackpot. It cost 11 cents to go to the movies, where they showed Westerns on Saturday mornings.

My younger sister Mary Clair frequently used to follow us to the grandstands on our treasure hunts. One day she found a dollar, and called out with excitement as she held it up. We all started to chase her down, but nobody could catch her. She had athletic talent of her own that would blossom later.

Watching sports that was all around us, and playing on the fields and in the gyms was our escape from the chaos of seven people living in a three-room shotgun house. That sports environment was like a gift to us. We didn't grow up with many advantages, but having fields and courts to play on and teams to learn from certainly was one. Sports also was the way that, as poor kids, we could blend in.

If we had stayed in the country and grown up around combines and hay balers, we'd probably have been good farm boys. But we grew up seeing sports and learning sports. If you threw us a football, we could catch it. We could play any position in baseball. We could dribble and shoot a basketball. When we were choosing sides down at the elementary school, the Langley boys always got picked. That was an important thing. For kids at our level in life, fitting in at school was about the hardest thing we did.

Chapter 12: Peer pressure

Our parents weren't involved in our schooling. They didn't go to programs or to open house. There were no meetings with teachers, no knowledge of what subjects we needed to work harder on. We brought our report cards home, and our mother didn't know whether we'd gotten an A or a B or a C: she'd just sign the report cards and we would carry them back. Our mother couldn't help us with things like school work or studying and never asked about our grades or what we were learning.

That lack of involvement by parents wasn't uncommon for the kids from Beasley Town. When they got to seventh, or eighth, or ninth grade, a lot of them would just quit school so they could get a job. The way they had grown up, most just wanted to make some money and feel just a little more in control.

I remember the kids whose parents were in the PTA and went to school activities. I remember watching other kids getting dropped off and picked up after school, and seeing the cars that carried them. I remember thinking at the time that they were not on the same path that I was on. Even at that age I could tell which of my classmates was college bound, and who wasn't.

It wasn't hard for us to see that those kids had advantages in school that we didn't have. But for the four older Langley kids, we knew that if we stayed in school we could play sports, and feel less like outsiders.

I was getting more confident about playing sports, but I was beginning to worry about my eyesight. As early as fourth grade, I couldn't see the blackboard at school. I didn't want anybody to know that my eyes

Bobby's school photo, 1951

were getting bad. I was starting to notice girls so I didn't want to wear glasses anyway.

One day I couldn't see the board, and there was a girl standing up in front of me. I asked her to sit down but she wouldn't, so I put my hand on her head to push her down.

The principal, Mr. L.I. "Bull" Mills, happened to be stalking the halls at that very moment and looked into the classroom as I pushed her down into her chair. He didn't say anything to the teacher, he just came in and slapped me hard right across the face then said, "boy, don't you do that again."

Though I respected Mr. Mills and even liked him, the effects of that slap stayed with me. Public shame was something that I already had too much of in my life. I didn't like the feeling of shame and I did what I could to avoid it. I dwelled on that incident for a long time.

Franklin Elementary was first grade through grade 8, but that was about to change. They were building a new school – Franklin Junior High – that I would be going to as soon as I finished fifth grade.

As construction began it occurred to me that kids who had been walking to Franklin Elementary might now be walking by my house to get to the new school on Fairground Street.

Lots of kids walked to school in those days, and I felt a sense of panic that was becoming familiar. I'd been flirting with some girls and I was afraid they were going to find out where I lived, even though most probably knew. I worried all summer. In fact, my worry about people finding out about my family and the way things were for us seemed to become ingrained over the years – trying to cover it up practically became an involuntary response.

But all my worry was for nothing.

Kids had been taught not to go through my neighborhood because it was black and poor white trash. So other than the local kids, I never saw a classmate passing by.

Nothing could have pleased me more.

Chapter 13: A look at another world

Late in the 1940s we finally got a radio. We would sit outside and listen on Saturday nights to the Grand Ole Opry and sing along with the songs. We still had no electricity: the radio was battery powered. When the battery would get low, mama would put it on the stove and warm it up.

I remember the smells of that time as we sat outside: coal smoke, fried potatoes, white beans, cornbread.

The food and the other smells are still in my head as warm memories. But I thought too much about some things, and thought about what other people might be thinking about me and my family. So sometimes even the good things, like food that I loved, got twisted around in my mind.

Billy Henry Warren, front, and from left, Robert King, Hubert Lee Bobby, Jimmy Cook and J.T. at The Ritz, a clubhouse for kids provided and maintained by the Asa and Margaret Jewell family.

I knew that just two blocks away at the Jewell house, they didn't eat the kind of food that we ate.

I met Asa Jewell, Jr. and the other three Jewell children while walking to school. His father, Asa senior, was a Kentucky native and was a partner with his brothers in the Jewell Tobacco Warehouse, a successful brokerage for burley tobacco in Williamson and Maury counties.

His mother, Margaret Jewell, was from Maine, and met Asa senior as the two were students in Boston. The background of this family was practically inconceivable to me, but Margaret Jewell became another one of those important influences on my life.

One day after school Asa Jr. invited me to his house to play. After playing outside for a while, he invited me inside the house for a Coke. This was a big event for me. Margaret Jewell greeted me with a smile, and I knew I truly was welcome in her home. The home couldn't have been more different from mine. It was the biggest house I had ever seen. In addition to beautiful furnishings, there was a black lady there named Frances who was cook and housekeeper for the Jewells. Frances was not just a worker, but truly was treated as part of the family.

I used to lay in bed and think about why my life was the way it was, and why other people, like the Jewells, lived the way they did. I thought about it more, I think, than other kids, and more than my brothers and sisters. I don't know why.

But Margaret Jewell had a lot of character, and cared about people from where I lived. I learned over time that she wanted to show me things and teach me that I could work my way out of my situation if I wanted to.

One afternoon during fall in the late 1940s Asa and I, along with Billy Speck, Abner Alley, "Buck" Beard and Grady Wray were playing football in the back yard at the Jewell house. We took a break to go in the house for water, and as we were headed back outside Mrs. Jewell pulled me aside and asked me if I would like to have dinner with them that night.

This was something I had never experienced, and in my excitement I said "yes" right away.

She said, "Bobby, you run home and ask your parents if it is OK with them."

I took her very literally and started running home as fast as I could. I remember my heart beating hard as I approached our house and saw my mother taking the wash off the clothesline.

I was out of breath and tugged at her apron saying, "Mama, mama, Mrs. Jewell asked if I could have dinner with them tonight."

"Dinner?" she asked. "Why, Bobby, you had dinner at school."

"Oh, no Mama, you don't understand. They call supper dinner."

"Well, they might, but we don't. And by the way, people who talk like that are way too uppity for you," she said, and then told me to ask my daddy.

My father was inside, sick again and resting in bed. I pleaded my case with him and he finally told me to go ahead, but come home right after supper.

Just after I got back to the Jewell house, Frances was leaning out the back door calling for Asa and I to come in and wash up. In the dining room I was dazzled by the big table with all the plates, silverware, cloth napkins and chandelier hanging above it all.

Mrs. Jewell sensed my fear and made sure that I was seated next to her. Nothing that Frances served was anything I had ever eaten before. I wasn't excited about that: I was horrified. The meal started with a bowl of oyster soup and got worse from there. I was trying my best to let Mrs. Jewell and Frances think I was enjoying it, but I'm not sure that I pulled it off.

I also was beginning to worry about how long it was taking. There was lots of conversation, unlike my house where meals were about eating. Mrs. Jewell wanted all her children to go over the events of the day during the meal. Finally it was over. I thanked Mrs Jewell for inviting me, and took off running again for home.

My father was in bed reading a newspaper when I got home. I said I was sorry for being late, and that dinners at the Jewells take a lot longer than suppers. He smiled and said, "That's OK, son. I hope you had a good time."

Chapter 14: Boy Scouts, paper routes

My father was still working at the cab stand, and also had begun driving a little. The owner of the cab company, Mr. Ragan, also took the job as the Franklin circulation manager for the *Nashville Banner* and *The Nashville Tennessean* newspapers.

That offered my brothers a chance to make a little money. As we all got older, we needed more clothes, and we also wanted to help with things around the house.
So in 1949, Hubert Lee and J.T. got paper routes. They got bicycles from Moody's Tire and began delivering the Tennessean every morning and the Banner in the afternoons.

At some point during the winter my brothers and I were asked to join the Boy Scouts. Mr. Billy Billington was the scoutmaster of Troop 135 and we met in the basement of St. Paul's Episcopal Church down at Five Points.

Mr. Billington had grown up at Riverside Plantation in Franklin and had been a fighter pilot in World War II.

We enjoyed the camaraderie with the other boys, but when we were asked to buy uniforms, we knew it wasn't going to be long before we would have to quit the scouts.

We still were hanging in there by summer, when we were invited to go to Camp
Boxwell, a scout camp then near McMinnville where boys would spend a week in the summertime swimming and working on merit badges.

I'm not sure why, but I was picked out of the bunch by Mr. Billington to go, I guess because my brothers and I acted right. We had manners. We weren't going to cause a problem or show off.

I don't know who paid for it, maybe Mr. Billington did.

J.T. had to stay home and carry the papers.

My mother didn't understand any of that. She didn't know anything about Boy Scouts or summer camp.

Mr. Bill Miller who owned the Buick dealership volunteered to drive some of the boys up there with his son, Tommy. He told me he would pick me up at my house, which brought on that familiar sense of panic.

I didn't want people to see my house, and I was becoming good at coming up with instant solutions supported by vague lies to keep them away. I told Mr. Miller that I had some other things to do first and would meet him in front of Franklin High School.

My week at Camp Boxwell was a good one – I felt relaxed as just one of the boys. But when Mr. Miller picked us up and drove us back to Franklin. I was getting worried again about him seeing my house, and maybe he sensed that. He dropped me and my paper sack full of clothes at the high school without even asking.

My second camping experience was at Cove Lake in western Williamson County.
All the scout leaders took us, including Mr. Bull Mills, the Franklin Elementary principal who had slapped and humiliated me when I was in fourth grade.

Some of the boys were really into the Boy Scouts big time, and had sleeping bags, tents, and uniforms. Like me, Billy Speck was in a situation where he would have to leave when it came time to get a uniform. We didn't have sleeping bags either, just a couple of blankets, and certainly no tent. As the other boys were setting up their camping gear, Billy Speck and I went to the lake to skip rocks. We caught a bullfrog as big as a hard hat.

Mr. Bull Mills and I got along, even after he slapped me that day in class. I knew that discipline was part of his job, but I told Billy Speck that I knew what I was going to do with that bullfrog. I had seen where Mr. Mills had set up, and put his sleeping bag, and I drifted over there and zipped the frog inside.

In the evening we sat around the fire and did all the Boy Scout stuff: singing songs, telling ghost stories.

Sometime later the fires died down and everyone went to bed. A short time later came a shout from Mr. Bull Mills, who thought the frog was a snake. He tore up tents and kicked fires and knocked over pots and pans getting out of that sleeping bag.

I told Mr. Mills many years later that I was the one who had done that. I had gotten my revenge on Bull Mills for slapping me.

Chapter 15: Christmas basketball

Hubert Lee, like our father, was a restless person, and he quickly got tired of doing the paper route.

That was my entry into the paper boy business, and I got to take over helping J.T. run papers all over northern Franklin and into the black Hard Bargain neighborhood before and after school. It was a pretty good distance from Granbury Street down to the square, then all of the route, then back up High School hill to get home before school. As we earned money, it became our mission to help our mother, and to help the family have things that we couldn't have before.

Our mother was doing the best she could to keep our clothes clean and keep food on the table. Like sports, dressing better and having pocket money from our paper routes also helped us to fit in better with our friends and the community around us.

I remember times when my mother cried that she couldn't get us anything for Christmas. It didn't bother us boys. We didn't care. My dad wasn't someone who got excited about Christmas either. But we cared that our mother cared and our paper route helped us make Christmas better with a few gifts, including ones that we bought for ourselves.

The church also would bring us things. Families would come around with gifts for my mother. They'd have the kids in the car and we would see them. It was very uncomfortable for us if they happened to be classmates.

For years that affected how I felt about Christmas. We didn't want to have to deal with that. It was hard at home, and hard at school. We would have to draw names at school and buy stuff. In school it seemed like there was always something that you had to spend money on, even if you didn't really have the money to spend. And it is so in schools today.

We didn't go anywhere for Christmas, and there wasn't even a visit from Papa Gene. I never remember him coming to Granbury Street. He still wasn't happy with my dad or his marriage. And he had his plate full raising another six children. Plus, they were still worried about tuberculosis with us.

My mother would always cook a hen for Christmas, and I remember my younger sister Carolyn coming to get us in the gym, to come home for Christmas dinner. We spent much of our Christmas holiday from school playing ball in the BGA gym. It always was available because the boarding students were not there.

Christmas holidays or not, any chance we had to get out of our small, crowded house, we took, and most of the time we were playing basketball – especially me. The BGA gym was left open and at 10 and 11 years old I spent hours over there by myself practically every day. I was really learning the game of basketball. If someone was in there, and it was someone I was comfortable with, I might play a pickup game, even with the BGA high school students. They would have to leave to study, and I would stay behind and practice. It would be getting late and I should have been home studying, but I would stay, shooting basket after basket from all over the court.

Lots of times my skinny little sister Mary Clair would tag along. She developed into a great athlete and basketball player, too.

Late in the evenings Mr. Akin would make his rounds, checking the fields for balls left lying around, books on the bleachers. And he could hear me in the gym bouncing the ball. He would stick his head in the door and say, "Bobby, make sure you turn the lights out before you go." That happened many times.

Even after we moved away from Beasley Town I would still go up there. I loved those old wooden backboards. Those old goals had soft spots on them. I loved that place and it still is in my heart today.

Chapter 16: Juba Lee

The Langley boys – and our sister, Mary Clair, were born and blessed with athletic ability. The better we got athletically, the more we fit in – with our Beasley town neighbors both black and white, and with the kids at school.

My oldest brother Hubert Lee may have been the best athlete among us. When I was nine and he was 12, he was the first one picked when choosing sides.

One day playing on a field at BGA, a boy asked us what our brother's name was. When we said Hubert Lee Langley, the boy dubbed him Jubilee, or Juba, for short. He was known by that all his life.

When the new Franklin Junior High opened, Hubert Lee started playing sports and enjoying success at it.

David Johnston, the junior high football, baseball and basketball coach, remembered Hubert Lee and the Langley children. We all had been fans of his when he was a star on the Franklin High baseball team and we would all watch the games at the County Center. With small towns as they are, Johnston also knew about the family situation.

Hubert Lee was a great player, but he always managed to get into a fight when we'd have a pickup game. He couldn't play very long without somebody poking him in the ribs. He didn't take it as part of the game, but would get into fights then end up going home.

Getting better at sports made me and most of my siblings feel more comfortable socially. But not Hubert Lee. Fitting in through sports only made him want to fit in other ways. Socially and economically, Hubert Lee was beginning to get out of his comfort zone. He was having a harder time in school, and possibly had learning problems inherited from our mother. My dad had no patience with him.

Just as Papa Gene was with him, my father was hard on his oldest son. One night Hubert Lee asked my dad to help him with his math. They sat down together and got to work, but Hubert Lee didn't seem to be getting it. After a while, my dad didn't think he was paying attention or trying, so he started slapping him and then grabbed a DDT sprayer and started beating him with it. When he finished beating him, you couldn't tell it was a fly sprayer.

Ironically, Hubert Lee had a lot of the traits and habits of my dad. He had a great personality and a lot of friends.

He didn't like the way we lived, but rather than work to improve things or accept things he could not change, he tried to fake it. He tried to act like somebody he was not, and tried to blend in with crowds of people that he should not have.

In trying to fit in with boys from families that were a lot different than ours, Hubert Lee had come to the point where he was lying all the time. He was being invited to do things that he couldn't afford, but somehow got the money.

In sports, Hubert Lee had it all. He had size, he could use his hands, he could play any sport. He was just a guy who could have been a star. But it caused him problems because he didn't know where to back off.

My brother J.T. and I watched that and learned about our limits and when to step back. I always thought Hubert Lee was a train wreck, and one day he would run off the track.

Chapter 17: Special delivery

The year 1951 dawned with a blizzard. Trees broke, power lines snapped. Our little wooden shotgun house was drafty in the best weather, and was even more than see-your-breath cold in a blizzard.

In the middle of all this, my father showed up at our house in a cab with chains on the tires. People were calling the cab company asking for food. He was up for the work, but because of his physical weakness, he needed help. He picked up my brothers and I to help him deliver meals from Clara Dotson's Snack Shop and Restaurant, the only thing open in the midst of the storm.

Even in normal times, part of the cab business in Franklin was delivering things. My father was well known, and those who knew him considered him trustworthy and discreet. He frequently would make purchases for some of the town's more distinguished residents who didn't want to be seen going into the liquor store.

The summer after the blizzard, Mr. Beasley put electricity into the shotgun houses, or at least enough to power one light bulb hanging down in the downstairs.

That same summer the news came that my father was going away again for another exploratory surgery. We thought at the time that it was just part of his care. We didn't know until later in life that he had volunteered to be a guinea pig for experimental surgery and research into TB.

It was always a relief when he was gone: no coughing, no anger, no arguments about drinking. He might be gone for three weeks or a month.

Without my father demanding peace and quiet all the time, we would have fun with our mother. After all these years, she still was a good dancer, thanks to my dad's efforts during their courtship. Many times we would get her to dance to the radio. She would do the Charleston and other dances of the 1930s. She would tell us about the dances that she would go to with my father during their courtship. I was always hugging her and kissing her, trying to make her happy, hoping to make her hard life positive.

It bothered J.T. and I that we were still on welfare, which we felt shamed and stigmatized by. We wanted to get out of the shotgun house, which the family had outgrown long ago.

As it was, our paper routes helped keep food on the table.

We decided to take the paper routes to another level. So we bought Allstate scooters, a brand built by Cushman and sold by Sears. The scooters allowed us to take on bigger routes, and the income not only paid for the scooters, but eventually earned us enough money to move to a better house.

In 1954, a house owned by Ms. Dorothy Lee, a teacher at Franklin Junior High, became available on Fairgrounds Street off Columbia Avenue. It wasn't a whole lot bigger than the Beasley Town house, but for the first time in Ruby Irene Langley's life she was going to have a house that had a bathroom, a commode, and hot and cold running water. It was a new life for the Langleys. J.T. and I told our dad that with the paper route money, we would pay the rent.

In time we got hold of a basketball hoop and nailed it to an old walnut tree in the yard. We spent many hours playing there, and we wore down the ground under the tree into a slick spot.

Now when someone at school asked where I lived, I said Columbia Avenue, even though it wasn't exactly on Columbia Avenue. I didn't want to say Fairground Street, because Fairground Street was a "black" street. Sometimes I felt guilty doing that because that wasn't the way to be … but that's the way it was.

Fairground Street was just a couple of blocks south of BGA, and I still went there to play. I also went to the County Center to play, and truly bonded through basketball with the best black players, including some who went on to be stars and hall of famers at Franklin Training School and Natchez High. They weren't welcome there when the white teams were playing, and because of that I always knew when they would be there.

Most of my time playing there, I played with people bigger than me, and older than me. I think that helped make me a better player.

Chapter 18: Playing up

Raymond "Buddy" Warren was my neighbor on Fairgrounds Street, and when we played baseball together around the neighborhood, he realized that I knew how to catch. Buddy was already a Franklin Junior High School student, and Coach Johnston had recognized his talent as a pitcher with the ability to throw a curve, or a drop, or a fastball.

When Coach Johnston needed a catcher to pair up with Buddy, my name came up. The coach was all for it. But because I was a sixth grader, he had to get special permission.

Our first game was against Trinity in eastern Williamson County. To this day I can remember how excited I was … and how scared I was. It must have showed because the coach came up to me and asked if I was scared, I said, "yes sir, I am."

But after Buddy's first pitch I knew it was going to go well. We won. It was the beginning of my career in organized sports. Coach Johnston had faith in me and I ended up starting in almost every game and catching for both Buddy and for John McCord, who would end up becoming a lifelong friend. John McCord lived on Fair Street, which was a world apart from Fairground Street. It was inhabited by comfortable families in stylish Craftsman and elegant Victorian homes. But sports brought John and I together.

Sports is where I found the success I needed to lift my spirit out of the hopelessness that often sunk other young people in my situation.

When I moved on to the seventh grade Coach Johnston had moved on to Franklin High.

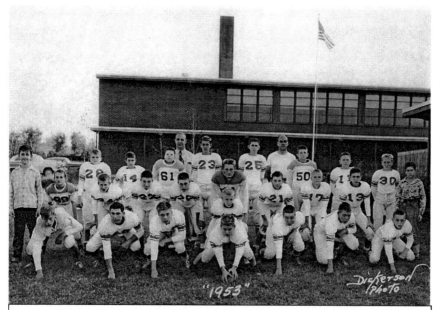

The 1953 Franklin Junior High School football team included Hubert Lee, the second boy behind Ray Dalton, the center, and Bobby, wearing number 30.

Still, I went out for football and made the team. Hubert Lee was in eighth grade and he was the best one on the team. He liked to brag on me to the other players who were bigger. We won all of our games.

Hubert Lee also was the Junior High's best basketball player. Of course, I went out for basketball as well. After hours and hours of practice over the years, I was a good shooter but I was still small. I became a guard on the basketball team.

In baseball, I played catcher sixth, seventh and eighth grade. We didn't lose a game the whole three years I went to Franklin Junior High.

In my eighth grade year I was a running back on the football team, and was a starter in every sport. I was setting the stage for what happened in high school.

The 1954-55 Franklin Junior High basketball team included athletes who went on to more success in sports, such as, from left, Billy Speck (No. 3), Bubba McMillan (7), Wayne Irwin (11), Ray Dalton (5), Bobby Langley (4), and Ned Sullivan (F).

Mary Clair, who was two years behind me, was setting her own stage. She was probably the best athlete in my family. Of course in those days, basketball was the only sport they had for girls and she sure made the best of it.

Neither one of our parents had seen any of us play, but I would watch Mary Clair's games, and she would watch mine. We were beginning to notice all the parents that would come and hang around the fence – even for practices. There were parents that were so involved with their kids that they couldn't help sticking their nose in their business or the coach's business when it came to sports. And it seemed to us there were coaches who showed favoritism to some kids because their parents were so and so in town. I'm not sure I envied or pitied the kids whose parents followed them so closely – probably a little of both.

The onset of adolescence gave me a whole new set of concerns about fitting in, about having the right clothes, about having money and having the respect of not just my friends, but of girls. I felt in control playing sports, but nowhere else in my life.

I was beginning to feel negative about school, and anxious about whether I could hold my own academically, at least so I didn't get labeled a dummy or get forced into a humiliating situation. Because of all these associated problems I had to solve, I was developing the attitude that school was a bunch of crap, but I wanted to do it and get it over with.

All through junior high I was balancing school, sports, and the paper route that we needed to pay the rent, the light bill, and buy coal oil. Bluntly, it was just a pain in the ass.

I still remember how hard it was to get up every morning and do the route before school, when the paper boys and the milkmen were the only activity on the streets. We had to run the afternoon paper route after practice for whatever sport I was involved in.

Another difficult thing to deal with was the abuse dealt by my father at home from time to time. One day I came home from school to find my mother with two black eyes. I loved her very much and that was one of many days that I felt pain on her behalf.

But by that age, I knew that I wasn't the only one growing up in such an environment. I also knew that there were so many kids that lived practically in another world, who had total support from their parents, and didn't have to worry about working for family necessities. It was hard and it forced me into a pattern – a defense mechanism – that I came to regret.

I decided that I was going to make school as easy as possible. I was going to take the easiest classes I could get away with. I had to get passing grades to play sports. I knew I could be a success in sports, but with my mother's situation hanging over me, I wasn't sure that I could always succeed in academics. Plus, it was embarrassing enough to be poor. I didn't need the humiliation of school failure on top of that.

Chapter 19: The family grows

At one point during my junior high years, we began to reconnect with my father's family and his half siblings. Papa Gene's "second" family was getting older, and he wasn't quite as worried about TB as he once was. My father had gotten well enough again to drive a cab, and we would visit the farm in the cab from time to time.

There was Aunt Jean, born in 1929; Aunt Mary, born in 1932; Uncle Pete (Alvin), born in 1935; Uncle Buck (Thomas), born in 1936; Aunt Nellie Joe, born in 1939, and Aunt Wanda, born in 1942. As we got to know them we came to realize that the great character of Mama Lela – who had shown such kindness to my mother when she was young and scared and living at the Holland-Langley place – was instilled in all of them.

Fertility must have run in the Langley family, because late in 1953 my mother wound up pregnant again. Ronnie Merrell Langley was born on Aug. 20 1954, the sixth child of Tyree and Ruby Langley. I was 14.

Having a baby in the house of course was complicated and expensive, but in many ways was just what the family needed at the time. Ronnie was an injection of joy and excitement, a focus of love for my family. For my mother it must have been difficult, but all of the children made it a positive thing and pitched in all the time.

As Beasley Town once was our world and our home, between our growing prowess in sports and our years delivering papers, our world now encompassed most of Franklin. We pretty much knew everyone, and could leave Fairground Street and go downtown and never see anybody we didn't know. A wave from the side of the road would get you a ride and some conversation.

We also knew where everybody lived. We knew all the police, the sheriff's deputies, the highway patrolmen. They would catch me driving my scooter on sidewalks and running stop signs, and chew me out and threaten to tell my dad. Just across from the newspaper office was West Point Restaurant, which was gossip central, so most of the time we knew more than we needed to know about what was going on in town.

Chapter 20: Sports town

When 1955 came around it was time for me to go to high school, and it scared me to death. I didn't have any self-confidence about the academics part, and I felt intimidated, even about sports. I had watched great teams play for Franklin High School for years. Now I was there, and I felt very small compared to the upperclassmen.

My brothers J.T. and Hubert Lee were there, but Hubert Lee was close to quitting school. He had been held back a few times and by now was in the same grade as J.T. Hubert Lee was frustrated with life, and my parents were frustrated with him. He wasn't always honest and he had become sort of a "wild child." He still wanted to be a big deal, and went down the wrong path because he couldn't face what we were in life or where we had come from. It was hard to see him spinning out of control.

He was down on himself mentally, but he didn't want to show it. He also didn't want to ask for help in school. My father had many talks with Hubert Lee. I think that he finally was beginning to realize that Hubert Lee was going down a path similar to the one that he had chosen.

In my freshman year I made the basketball B-team, a notch above the freshman team. There was a lot of small town politics in sports at that time, and a lot of competition. At the high school level you had kids coming in from all over the county, some were pretty good. Others had parents that were big in the business world, or important in politics. There were kids who were great at the middle school level who would go out for high school sports and get cut. I wasn't even sure about my own true talent level.

Franklin was a sports town. The newspapers in Nashville covered high school sports then like they do the pros today. BGA and Franklin High had stars that were known all over the region.

I felt a lot of pressure to perform, and a lot of stress from balancing school, sports, and our paper routes.

Paper boy Bobby Langley poses on his Cushman scooter.

JT and I had gotten bigger scooters: Cushman Eagles, and bigger paper routes. We would have to suit up for football practice after school, then rush off to do our afternoon paper routes. When basketball season arrived, it was the same. Mr. Ragan was always mad about that.

I didn't go out for baseball that year because my eyes were getting bad. I probably had needed glasses since the third grade, but I didn't have the money and I didn't want to do it anyway. Kids made fun of you in those days if you had glasses.

I missed playing, but it was a relief to get away from Mr. Ragan's harshness for a few months about sports and paper routes.

Chapter 21: Jukebox and a hamburger

I was making $20 a week from my paper route: about as good as it got for paper boys in those days. The income was a big help for my mother and daddy, and it also allowed me to pay for my lunch at school, and buy some clothes. I also picked up another job at a Shell station owned by two members of the Herbert family from Brentwood. During the summer I worked there every day.

In many ways I was glad to be out of the little shotgun house near BGA, but I never really got Beasley Town out of my heart, and now know how important that part of my life was to the path I followed. Sometimes I would just ride my Cushman through Beasley Town to see the old house, the old neighbors. I'd ride down Carter Street to see my black buddies and go to Porky's Store. I would go back to the old gym at BGA to shoot baskets or play pickup games, or spend some time playing at the County Center. As busy as I was, I'd always find time to go shoot basketball.

With pocket money and transportation, I was beginning to feel like I was fitting in to the big world beyond family and neighborhood. Plus, the '50s was an exciting time to be a teenager with the cars, the music and the culture. We had our own "American Graffiti" scene centered around the hamburgers and jukebox of the Gilco Drive-In out on Lewisburg Avenue. Sometimes I'd ride my Cushman Eagle down there just to see if there were any girls there that I was sweet on.

Not far from The Gilco was Willow Plunge, a swimming pool that I would go to in the summertime after my morning paper route. I'd stay until it was time to do my afternoon deliveries. I remember thinking that the girls there had to be the prettiest in the world.

I learned a lot as a paper boy, and had a lot of adventures and a few mishaps. Once I launched a paper through a picture window, which

I had to replace. Another time I wasn't paying enough attention and hit Mr. William Garrett's brand new 1955 Oldsmobile. The papers went flying from my satchel. Mr. Jake, the barber, saw the crash and came out of his shop to ask if I was OK. Then he told me to pick up the papers and go, he would take care of it. I'm not sure what he meant by that, but I was sure grateful to him. I avoided Mr. Garrett for the rest of his life.

The paper boys were all from families where the boys needed to work to pay their own way. We were a close-knit bunch of boys who would do things together. The Nashville Tennessean would have contests to raise circulation, and the winners would get to go to the big pool in Nashville, Cascade Plunge, near the state fairgrounds. The paper boys sometimes would go to the bowling alley in Melrose, or hang out at the chocolate shop up there.

One Sunday morning – Jan. 29, 1956 – I was going down high school hill when there was a monstrous blast of lightning that lit up the sky like daylight. It was so loud and so close that I pulled my Cushman up on the sidewalk. J.T. had left before me and was all the way down the hill at thc corncr drugstore at the time. After my heart slowed down to normal I got back on the road and then went to get my papers. When I got up on Everbright Street, heading back toward the high school, I could see smoke billowing. I had just run out of papers so I needed to go back down the hill. The scene was chaos. Franklin High School was on fire and people were trying to get things out. The 1926 building was a total loss, though the new gym, just completed in 1954, was saved, along with the Agriculture department out back.

So after growing up in the shadow of the old school, I only got to go there half of my freshman year. Afterward the gym and the ag department were split into classrooms, and classes also were held in the churches downtown.

Chapter 22: Sideline smackdown

When my sophomore year arrived, J.T. and Hubert Lee were going to be juniors. J.T. and I went out for football. I had to go to football camp at Montgomery Bell State Park for almost a week, which cost $25. J.T. didn't go, and covered my paper route for me. I covered his routes the following year for him.

Hubert Lee also started the season off. But it wasn't long before he was having trouble in class again. This time he decided to quit school join the Navy.

His troubled young life had affected the whole family. Sometimes it seemed like he got along with everyone on earth except us. It was our hope that he would find his place in the world by joining the Navy.

My mother and father signed the papers to let him enlist, and soon he was ready to ship out for boot camp in San Diego.

The day we took him to the airport in Nashville to leave was a hard one for my mother. This was her firstborn and their bond was strong.

Hubert Lee Langley, USN

Unlike Hubert Lee, J.T. and I were pretty committed to sticking with school, me mostly for sports.

We kept carrying the papers and playing football, which didn't sit well with Mr. Ragan, who cussed us every day because our afternoon papers were delivered to customers later than usual. J.T.

and I just took it. We never said much but just picked up our papers and went on our way.

But one day at practice Mr. Ragan pulled up in one of his taxicabs. I saw him out of the corner of my eye. He motioned for me to come over to the car. I took my helmet off and walked toward him.

Mr. Ragan quickly raised his voice, demanding to know whether it was going to be football, or the paper routes. He started talking about what kind of family I came from and said that I needed to work, not play. He shouted, "are you going to play this stupid ass game of football, or are you going to carry those papers like you need to be doing?"

Standing not far away was his son, Wayne Ragan, who was the starting quarterback.

If I ever had a chance to play out that scene from my life again, I would have stomped his ass right there in front of the world.

But I was raised never to talk back to older people, and though a few of my teammates were watching him dress me down, I kept quiet. After all, there were other kids who loved sports and even had talent, but they couldn't work it out. Either they couldn't find a way home from practice, had chores or crops and livestock to tend, of they just had no support from their parents and couldn't play.

Still, after Mr. Ragan yelled at me that day, I left practice, went to the gym, took of my gear and never played football again. I couldn't deal with it. Mr. Ragan was right: my family needed the money that the paper routes brought.

But I was going to play basketball come hell or high water.

J.T. stayed with football, which he had a particular talent for. When we were kids in Beasley Town we would hang out at the

BGA practice field and a couple of the players there had taught him how to kick. He had developed into a great left-footed punter.

In fact, J.T. was one of the best punters that Franklin High had ever fielded, once kicking 62-yards against West High School in Nashville to win the game and the championship.

One day Mr. Ragan came to practice and tried the same thing with him – chewing him out in public – but J.T. wasn't going to quit football. I helped cover his routes for him when he needed me to.

Still, for all the unkindness that came our way, there was an equal measure of kindness. Another special person that stands out is Mr. Herbert Clouse, a cab driver who had left Mr. Ragan and operated his own cab as a one-man show. We didn't own a car, and once when J.T. asked a girl for a date, my dad asked Mr. Clouse if J.T. could borrow his cab. J.T. ended up picking up his girl in that cab.

Mr. Clouse was a great friend of our whole family, but not too long after that he was murdered out in the country on Jordan Road in a case that never was solved.

Chapter 23: Standing up for the boys

Once again my father was smoking too much, drinking too much, and working too much at the cab company. But just as he had worked out the deal for J.T. to borrow Mr. Clouse's cab, he also stood up for us in other ways.

One Halloween night some young BGA boys were out trick or treating and ran into some Franklin High boys. There was a long history of sports rivalries that usually resulted in trash talk or pranks, but this night the two groups got into a big rumble. The BGA boys ended up on the losing end of the fight.

One of the BGA boys accused the Langley boys and a few others of doing it, and told Headmaster Paul Reddick. He came up to Franklin High and asked Principal Barry Sutton to get J.T. out of shop class.

Ruby, Tyree and J.T. pose at the house on Fairgrounds Street.

When J.T. showed up at the office with some of the other suspects, Mr. Reddick went straight for J.T. He started shouting, shoved J.T. up against a wall and jabbed his finger into J.T.'s chest. J.T. didn't know what he was talking about.

Later a Franklin High student went to BGA and apologized on behalf of the school for the brawl.

That night after supper, J.T. told my dad what had

happened. My dad knew that it wasn't us who had beaten up the BGA students. We had been good kids and had not caused any problems. He also probably suspected that J.T. got the worst treatment because we had no status in the community.

After supper my dad looked at me and said, "Bobcat, come on and go with me." I wasn't sure where he was going.

He drove to the headmaster's residence and told me to get out of the car and go up to the door with him. He knocked on the door and Mr. Reddick answered it, and came out on the front porch.

My dad was thin and weak because of his tuberculosis, but that night he was boiling with anger and was standing tall and strong. He told Mr. Reddick that he had heard what had happened and that it was wrong. Then he said, "If you want to keep this fine house, don't ever lay a hand on any of my children again."

There were times I wasn't proud of my dad, but I was proud he was my dad that night.

Chapter 24: Practice pays off

When basketball season came around, I'd been practicing and was in shape for it. I was determined to make that team, and I did.

A lot of times in the South, football was king. Basketball ranked a distant second and a lot of times the assistant football coach was the basketball coach. Frequently, that led to football players seeing a lot of action in basketball not for the sake of winning in that sport, but just to help them stay in shape all year round.

My old friend Coach David Johnston was a fair man and didn't give the football players priority. His basketball team was assembled strictly on merit. The seniors that year were some of the best players ever, so at first I wasn't sure I would even make the team.

I also worried that my having walked off the football team after the incident with Mr. Ragan would be held against me. Both Coach Johnston and Principal Sutton asked me about what happened on the football team. When I explained, they understood. Both knew that I wanted to play basketball most of all.

 J.T. didn't play basketball, so he could cover my paper routes for me when I was at games.

Basketball season did not start off well. Coach Johnston started coming up with all these complicated offenses that were hard for the team to learn. There was the "Auburn shuffle," and the "Drake shuffle." We were supposed to pass three times before shooting. He would change up the starters, and move players among positions. It seemed that he was torn between being a teacher and being a coach – between teaching us about the art and science of basketball and just winning games. We were intimidated by his coaching and felt like we didn't have any freedom to exploit sudden weaknesses in the opponent.

But this team had the potential to be great, and Coach Johnston eventually recognized that.

After weeks of confusion, practice eventually became free throw contests, or one-on-one games. That's when Coach Johnston began to see the results of how much time I had put into the game of basketball. I was 5' 10" playing against guys 6' 3" and I'd beat the crap out of them.

Toward the end of the season he did away with all the exotic stuff that he had tried. He found out there was one guy on that team who could shoot, and it was me. The last four or five games of the year, he had me playing forward, with Wayne Whitehurst at the other forward, and Ken Frost at the middle.
Now we were doing fast breaks, Frost would get the ball off the boards and pitch it out to the middle. Finally we were winning games.

Despite our less-than-stellar start to the season, we got into the District Tournament. It was February, 1957, and was scheduled to be played in "the new gym," which was the only part of Franklin High to survive the fire.

There were some really good teams in our district, as well as in our region: Linden, Lawrenceburg, Summertown, BGA and Columbia Central. The odds were on Columbia to win the region and make it to state.

Franklin drew Columbia to play first. Columbia came to town ready to blow Franklin out and then to beat BGA. But I put their lights out: I was hotter than a firecracker and blew through their zone defense. I could jump, shoot, I had long arms. I scored 20 points against them. It was one of the best games of my life.

Though I finally felt validated and confident, I actually felt sort of sorry for Columbia because I knew how good they were. But my success in the game was a tonic: this game truly set the stage for me.

The next night we were up against BGA in the semifinals. I was hot again, and the game stayed close. But BGA was pretty hot, too, and ended up beating us by just two points.

We were out of the tournament, but I went back the next night to watch the finals.

Though I was in the crowd and not on the court, it was to be a very special night. I ran into Kathy Ashford, a girl that I had begun to like. Sometimes she would walk to class with me. She was one of the managers of the girls basketball team that had made it into the finals. We ended up sitting together. BGA took on Culleoka and beat them for the championship. Kathy and I were watching from a seat in the end zone as they presented the district trophy. Then they announced the all-district team, and to my surprise the announcer called out my name. I was the only sophomore on an all-district team of juniors and seniors.

Having Kathy Ashford sitting beside me when they called my name was electrifying. And things just got better from there. A guy who had a car came up to me and asked if Kathy and I would like to go to the Gilco Drive-in with him and his girlfriend. So the night I made the All-District team also was the first time I was in a car with a girl on a date. It was a very good night.

Chapter 25: Four eyes

I still needed glasses. During the basketball season I couldn't even tell what the score was.

 I didn't know how much glasses would cost. But I knew I was going to have to deal with it.

Coach Johnston asked me to come out for baseball. I didn't want to because of the paper route and because I couldn't see, but I said yes. I couldn't hit very well any more. But I ended up starting almost every game and doing pretty well. Buddy Warren had a great season. One day he struck out 18 batters, a league record. That was the last year I ever played any organized game of baseball.

By the end of my sophomore year I was pretty well pleased with what I had done in sports. But to me at that time, school was still a pain in the ass, a high price to pay for pursuing my basketball passion. I wasn't passionate at all about school work: I still was afraid to fail, afraid to look like a dummy. So I tried to keep it simple.

One day that summer I decided I was making enough on the paper route to finally deal with my eyesight. I went to see Dr. Robert Sullivan, the eye doctor in Franklin. After he tested my vision he said "you don't play sports, do you?"

When I told him that I did, he said he couldn't understand how I could have played with my eyesight.

He showed me pictures of sports glasses and street glasses. I was really concerned about how I was going to look. He ordered the regular glasses and then, at the end of the summer, he ordered my sports glasses, and told me that it would by fine to "pay a little bit along."

It was a new world when Dr. Sullivan fitted those glasses. Suddenly I didn't care how I looked. I got laughed at, but I didn't care. The world had just opened up to me. I knew it would help me in school.

When I showed up for work at the Shell station the guys called me goggle eyes, one told me I looked like "two piss holes in a snow bank."

Having good vision inspired a vision: it was during that summer that I decided I wanted to be the best basketball player in Williamson County. I knew what it would take to get there, and that's what I started doing. I would go to the County Center and shoot, shoot, shoot. Roy Apple and I became close friends and played basketball together a lot, going around town and finding pickup games.

Because I needed to pay for my sports glasses, I spent the summer working a lot and doing the paper route. But I didn't want to do the papers any more during basketball season. So before the season started I told Mr. Ragan I wasn't going to carry papers any more. Instead I was working at the service station on weekends for $5 a day. It seemed like everything was falling into place.

Hubert Lee got on one of the Navy Special Services basketball teams in the Pacific islands and ended up touring around, winning tournaments. That summer he came home to visit. One day he suggested we go to the County Center for some one-on-one basketball. He beat the crap out of me. He was 19 and I was 16. He had talent galore and had wasted it in high school. But he brought me down to earth that day and taught me that I would have to really work hard to achieve my goal of being the best.

The better life got for us, and the more we saw how people lived around us, the more ashamed we felt of my mother's family. They were poor and uneducated, but had given our family a lot of support over the years. These days we didn't see them much. Even my mother, who now kept a spotless house, was embarrassed about the dirty conditions her family lived in.

When Tyree wasn't around, Ruby and the kids would dance and play, such as on this occasion when Bobby joked that the dancing had caused him to lose his underpants.

Papa John had left the Werthan Farm and now was living and working at the Carmichael farm, where Nathan Bedford Forrest's horse Roderick is buried, just north of Thompson's Station.

Uncle Bug was taking care of the horses at the farm, mucking out stalls and so forth. Uncle James, crippled with braces on his legs, couldn't do much. Aunt Dorothy also was limited, but was passionate about her photography hobby. The only one of the Hammox children who really ventured out was Vester, the oldest sister. She ended up marrying a man who worked on the farm with Papa John, and together they raised a son, Wesley Eugene, who was named after Papa John Wesley Hammox. We all called the boy Sonny.

The Langleys still were living on Duplex Road on the family land. We didn't see them very much during those times either.

Chapter 26: Father figure

In the fall of 1957 another special person came into my life when Ernest McCord became the new assistant football coach at Franklin High School, and the designated basketball coach. The McCords were an old local family from Bethesda, which is close to Spring Hill in southern Williamson County.

Coach McCord was a lifetime educator who had been the coach at Franklin when I watched the team as a young boy. I knew who he was and he knew who I was. The chemistry was there: he loved basketball and I did too. Coach McCord eventually became the closest thing to a second father that I ever had.

He coached J.T. as line coach that fall in football, where they won the AA championship for second consecutive year.

But I had learned that in sports, there are football guys and there are basketball guys. A lot of times in those days (and sometimes today), the high school football guys thought they ran the sports world. Many times and in many places, football players were favored in every sport and were given starting roles just to keep them in shape for the football season. But that wasn't going to be true with Ernest McCord because he was a basketball guy.

With Coach McCord in place, the age of the domination of the Franklin football player was over. That fall, some of the football players who came out for basketball ended up leaving because they could not play at the level of basketball that was played by guys like Donald Frazier, Roy Apple, and me. We ended up with about 12 boys on the varsity squad that year.

Coach McCord's style had a lot of "backyard basketball" to it. He taught fundamentals, not fancy stuff. He taught great defense, and was a coach who let people play to their talents. If you had a weak man playing defense on you, you could tell a teammate to "set a pick" for you when you came down the court. Coach McCord would let the players on the court make calls, offering criticism only when those calls were wrong.

Co-captains Bobby Langley and Roy Apple of the 1957-58 Franklin Rebels basketball team

He made playing fun. He didn't scream, he didn't yell, and unlike some coaches, he didn't cuss the kids. He was the kind of coach that you wanted to give everything to. We started off doing pretty well that season.

Coach McCord also coached the girls team, including my sister, Mary Clair, who was a freshman that year.

Our team lacked a big post player, but had a lot of chemistry. Among the starters, Ray Dalton and Wayne Irwin were football players. Dalton was a playmaker, but not a shooter. Irwin, who was 6'1", was a good jumper, good shooter, and a good rebounder. Donald Frazier was one of the fastest players on a basketball floor and could run like a deer. The other two starters, Roy Apple, a senior, and me, a junior, were nominated to be co-captains.

In November of 1957 our new high school, built on part of the Cheek Farm a mile out of town on Hillsboro Road, finally opened. We played our last game against Hillsboro High of Nashville in the three-year-old gym on high school hill, next to the former site of Franklin High.

We were going to christen the new school's gym with a charity game for the March of Dimes against our old rival BGA. Students and parents helped move things over to the new school, and volunteers actually put the bleachers together in the new gym.

The highlight of the charity game for me was that I got to score the first points ever made in the new gym. Unfortunately, we ended up losing again to our rivals from BGA.

During Christmas break I would work in the Jewell Tobacco Warehouse and the Casey Tobacco Warehouse packing tobacco into barrels. It was hard work but it paid well. I also helped a little on the paper routes.

I felt a sense of momentum as 1958 began. My scoring average was going up and I felt like I was beginning to come into my own. All those hours I spent in the gym as a child were really paying off. My confidence – and my belief that I could achieve my goal of being the best – continued to grow.

I had sold my Cushman Eagle and frequently rode home from practice with Coach McCord. He was the kind of man I needed in my life at the time. I think it was a pleasure for him to watch kids grow and get better. We talked a lot on the rides home. He knew my basketball talents. He knew that I never took a shot that I didn't think I could make. We would talk about sports, and he would talk about "the game of life."

Coach McCord gave me plenty of advice, but I didn't take all of it, especially when it came to him encouraging me to study. I was running from something that I probably shouldn't have. I didn't know what basketball was leading to, but in school I was just doing enough to

Bobby spent hours and years in gyms and on outdoor basketball courts pursuing his goal to be the county's best basketball player.

get by. How wrong I was.

The new gym at Franklin High was attracting big crowds. Franklin had that small- town "Hoosier" flavor where lots of people would go to basketball games for the entertainment. People in town supported both BGA and Franklin, but those who followed the game knew who the players were on many of the opposing teams. When they would see the players on the street they would talk to them about the games, mention a good shot or play, or make small talk about the season.

With my growing reputation for scoring, opponents frequently showed up gunning for me.

Like the BGA sports rivalry, there also was a "city vs. country" rivalry between Franklin High and the country high schools. For years there had been a countywide tournament, but it had been discontinued because of an increase in fights and accusations of cheating among the schools.

Coach McCord wanted to revive the tournament to bring fans and money in, especially in Franklin's big, new gym. West Williamson, Hillsboro, College Grove, Bethesda and Franklin all agreed to meet again for the county tournament. We knocked them all off, until we ended up in the finals against West Williamson. It wasn't an easy game as I was up against Eugene Pack, a big country boy from Fairview who was 6'7" and was one of the best players I ever faced in high school. With me being not even 6 feet tall, Pack was hard to handle. But we ended up winning and I was voted MVP of the tournament.

We did pretty well at the district tournament, though that year Columbia Central beat us. I was named to the All-District Team for the second year in a row.

Chapter 27: Wheat harvest

My habit of doing the minimum to get by in school ended up interfering with my love life.

Legendary Franklin High English teacher Mary Trim Anderson knew what kind of student I was, and knew that because of my study habits and my family situation, college probably was not in the cards for me. She also knew that Kathy Ashford was a good student, and most likely was college bound. Word began to circulate that Ms. Anderson had shared this fact with Kathy's parents, possibly through Kathy's mother, who was a substitute teacher.

I never could confirm this with 100 percent confidence, but something happened and Kathy stopped seeing me.

I was wounded, and for a while thought about trying to go live with my Aunt Polly in Columbia, so I could play my senior year in basketball for Franklin's rival Columbia Central High School. Lucky for both of us, Kathy's father was transferred by his company to Tyler, Texas and they left after her junior year.

Instead of baseball junior year I went out for track that spring. I wanted to stay in shape. I ran the 880 yard dash and was on the two-mile relay team. Our track team was pretty strong that year and I did pretty well and made a good showing at the Banner Relays.

J.T. was about to graduate as part of the class of 1958. He was the first person in the family to graduate from high school. I was really proud of him, and proud of what he had accomplished in sports. My mother didn't go to his graduation, though my father did.

Without my paper route, I had begun to worry about what I was going to do that summer. An idle summer vacation was not something that I could conceive of. I had worked since I was 9 years old.

I started talking to Robert Inman and Wayne Inman, two of my paper boy buddies who had gone out to Caldwell, Kansas and worked in the wheat harvest the past three years. I'd never traveled and was still stinging from the Kathy Ashford breakup, so this appealed to me, as did the money.

Wayne Inman didn't want to go again. But the wheat farmer, Ed Ziba, called him and asked if he could come again. Wayne asked me and Roy Apple to go, and we said yes right away.

My dad said I couldn't do it. But I just kept telling him how much money I could make: a dollar an hour. And not only that, there would be one less person to feed in the house. I finally talked him into it.

We called Mr. Ed Ziba and he told us how to get there. We were to take a bus to Wichita, and from there catch the train to Caldwell. We got the money to go, with part of it being a loan from Roy Apple's mother.

Coach McCord was not thrilled about my plans because he had been hoping I would spend the summer working on my game.

But I was ready for an adventure, ready to make some real money, and ready to get out of town and get Kathy Ashford out of my system.

Roy Apple's mother drove us to the bus station. We rode across Tennessee and Missouri, and half way across Kansas. We were glad to get off that bus, but not for long: right away a policeman stopped us for jaywalking. He started asking us questions about what we were doing, and I guess he decided we were sincere and harmless, because he decided not to write us a ticket.

That night we were sleeping in an old hotel when we were awakened by banging on the doors. The hotel people told us that there was a big tornado headed our way and that the safest place to go was the basement of the train station. That night – June 10, 1958 – we sheltered in the station as the Wichita area had one of the worst tornadoes in the city's history.

The trains still were running, though, and the next day we got a ticket on the Rock Island Line. A few hours later Mr. Ziba met the train in Caldwell and took us to his farm.

Our job was to stand by with trucks while the combines cut the wheat, then move the trucks into place each time a combine was ready to empty its load. After a truck was full, we would drive to the grain elevator to be weighed and unloaded before going back for more.

The wheat harvest was a huge operation conducted on enormous farms, and we worked from the time the sun dried the morning dew off the wheat until sundown, seven days a week if it didn't rain. Mr. Ziba's wheat was the first to be cut, then we moved around to other farms in Western Kansas and even into Eastern Colorado, cutting and hauling the wheat there.

We slept in barns, we slept in the trucks, and we even slept in bunkhouses if the farm had them.

The best part was the farm food: sumptuous midday dinners around big tables.

When it rained we'd go to town and play snooker and drink beer.

When the wheat was all in, we set off hitchhiking to visit Roy Apple's dad, who lived in Jackboro, Tex. After the visit we started hitchhiking east from Wichita Falls, Tex. It wasn't easy. We had to catch 35 or 40 rides before we ended up in Clarksville, Tenn., on the Kentucky state line outside of Fort Campbell. We couldn't get a ride for quite a while. But then a soldier came out of the main gate of Fort Campbell and he recognized us. Louis Ryan was from College Grove and he used to be a referee at middle school basketball games. He drove us all the way home to Franklin.

It was good to be back home. When I showed up my sister Mary Clair was playing basketball on our hoop mounted on a tree with a basketball that Coach McCord had dropped off. Ronnie, who was 4 going on 5 gave me a hug and said he had really missed me.

And now I was a year away from getting out of school: something I'd thought about since I was 10 years old. It was a wonderful and frightening thought: I'd be getting it over with at last … but didn't have a clear plan for what would happen after that. That was an unsettling feeling.

School had started a couple of days before we got back. When I went to school it seemed to have a really different feel. I'm sure having left town for the summer was part of it, but another thing was that a lot of the guys I had grown up with had graduated, like my basketball teammates Roy Apple, who was my age but had started school the year before I did, and Kenneth Mangrum, and my paper boy buddies Joey Davis and Billy Henry Warren. And my brother J.T. had graduated as well. I felt kind of lonely entering my senior year.

Chapter 28: Confession, consequences

As far as basketball was concerned, I felt fresh as my senior year began. I figured that it did me good to get away from something I'd been obsessed with much of my life. And I still had my game.

Coach McCord was putting in a new "V" offense and planned to use it both for the boys and for the girls. He asked me to teach it to the girls, including my sister Mary Clair.

But while my basketball world was secure, there was more stress in the family. Our finances were pretty bad. All of us kids were older, needed more stuff, and ate more. My mother and daddy had missed the income I had with that paper route and my dad and I had words about it more than once. His health seemed to be worse than ever, but he was working for the Thompson Cab company. Mr. Ragan was distributing newspapers fulltime, and Mr. Jim Thompson ran a Sinclair station, the Thompson Café, and the cab company.

My dad also got a job at the Williamson County Highway Department driving a truck hauling gravel. He had a hard time even climbing up into the cab of those big dump trucks, but sure needed the income.

My father maintained charge accounts at lots of little grocery stores around town, but kept getting his credit cut off because he often would use his money for alcohol instead of paying the grocery bill.

My sister Carolyn was struggling in school. She was skinny, frail and quiet, and had learning difficulties. She was frequently embarrassed and intimidated about her clothes.

Bobby Langley, center, wearing glasses and a white sweater, sits in Mary Trim Anderson's English class at Franklin High.

All around, it was a tough time for my family and for me. All the pieces that had fallen into place to make me feel confident and successful were falling apart. Though I never had applied myself enough in school, I really let my studies slide that fall. I failed history and then I failed English. That became a big problem.

Every six weeks a student had to turn in a book report. I don't think I read a book the whole time I was in high school. I would get other kids to tell me about books they had read, and write something up just to get by. I would choose books that a fifth grader would read. In the fall of my senior year I picked out a book that probably was a bit over my head and talked a girl in the class into writing the book report for me. I turned it in.

Ms. Mary Trim Anderson was no fool. She knew what the talents of various students were, and knew their boundaries. She came by my desk in class one day and said, "I want to ask you something and I want you to tell me the truth. Did you read that book?"

I looked up at her and said "No ma'am I didn't." She thanked me for telling the truth, and then gave me an F.

That meant that I was going to miss the beginning of the basketball season.

You couldn't fail two subjects and still play. I couldn't even practice with the players. I had been a top player in the spotlight and all of a sudden, I couldn't even sit on the bench. *The Nashville Tennessean* did a story about it, with a photo taken in the library with Coach McCord as I checked out a book.

I felt that the pressure was on like never before. For the first time in my life I buckled down in my studies and when the grades came out, I passed everything. I even made a few Bs.

My desire to get back on the basketball court had broken a barrier that I had built that kept me from studying for fear of failing. That report card was the first time I realized that I was capable of succeeding academically. I knew after that report card that I should have been studying harder all along, and that by taking the easy route for fear of failing, I had closed one of the doors to my future.

Even though my academic failure was all over the sports pages, my parents didn't know about my grades, or my basketball suspension. I never told them. Mary Clair, who was part of the basketball world, knew.

The Franklin Rebels had lost the five opening games, which made me feel terrible. I felt I had let the team down and I was ashamed of what I had done. I should have known that I couldn't get away with cheating with Mary Trim Anderson. And I also felt that I had let down my mentor, Coach McCord.

There was hope for the season, though. Just as I was ready to come back to basketball after my suspension, the football players who also played basketball were wrapping up their extended season. All five of our top starters were ready to go again, and we still had chemistry among us.

Of course, just when my year that started so poorly seemed to turning around, my oldest brother Hubert Lee got kicked out of the Navy and came home. I don't know what he did or what kind of trouble he got into. I didn't ask and didn't want to know. Once again the house was overcrowded, but that wasn't the only problem with his return. He quickly fell in again with a crowd that was steering him in the wrong direction.

But he did manage to get a job: Nashville Electric was a hard place to get hired, but Hubert Lee managed. He could talk his way into anything, or out of anything. But he wasn't dependable, and though he could dazzle people in the beginning, in the end he couldn't hold a job.

His return brought even more stress to the family.

Chapter 29: Hot streak

I didn't want to think about Hubert Lee. My basketball suspension was over and I was ready to play – really ready.

My first game back was against Lewisburg. It was big rivalry and an away game, but we beat them. Next we took down Mount Pleasant, Hillsboro, and then Hampshire. It felt good to be back and I knew this was going to be my ultimate season.

Coach Ernest McCord goes over a play with the Franklin Rebels basketball team

Coach McCord had come up with an idea for a basketball tournament during the Christmas holidays, and sold Principal Sutton on the idea. So in December of 1958 the first Middle Tennessee Invitational Tournament brought the top boys and girls basketball teams to Franklin High School.

Up until then, we had won all the games since I came back. We won our first game in the tournament, but then got knocked out. Once again, I made All-Tournament team.

In January 1959, I could tell that things were going well for me. I was focused both on basketball and on school.

Coach McCord and I still were talking a lot, and his advice on "the game of life" finally was beginning to sink in. He accepted a lot of the realities of my situation, and he could tell that I knew that and felt his support. He knew that I wanted to move on after school and get a job and start bringing home more money. I knew he was getting calls from colleges about me, but he kept a lot of that from me because he knew that with my grades and with my family situation, college probably wouldn't be possible.

He did help me get a taste of college basketball, though. Coach McCord was well-known in coaching circles, and was able to arrange scrimmages against college freshman teams Middle Tennessee State, David Lipscomb University, and Austin Peay, Those games were exciting and I scored well against the college teams.

A short time later Georgetown College in Kentucky invited me, Wayne Irwin, and other good basketball players from the Nashville Interscholastic League on a recruiting trip, and told us to bring our uniforms and shoes.

We played against their freshman team, I scored 20 points.

There were scholarship offers for me, including Georgetown, Austin Peay, and Belmont. Of course I didn't have the grades, nor did I have the means to ever seriously consider them, and it was frustrating.

I loved spending time with Coach McCord. I loved him and cared about him and felt like he cared about me, too. Sometimes he would get me out of study hall and we would just play one-on-one so he could watch me shoot and work with me. I never had that camaraderie with my dad because he was sick, and worked, and there were six kids. Coach McCord was a man that became a part of my life and remained a part of my life.

On Jan. 16, 1959, we were set to face archrivals Lewisburg again. Lewisburg had whipped our football team for years, and any time we played them it was a big game. Their players were known to be aggressive, and used wise cracks and trash talk as part of their strategy. Many of the players had been together since middle school days, so we were familiar with them and their style.

The gym that night was packed and the crowd was stoked by the rivalry atmosphere. It wasn't hard for Coach McCord to get us fired up. When the game got started, I could tell right off the bat that things were going well.

From the opening buzzer, there was something in the air. There was good chemistry among the team and I felt good, balanced, and controlled moving up and down the court. There was a beat, and a rhythm. Running our plays felt natural, reflexive. I was shooting well from the outside. I was sinking layups. The whole team was in synch, and we held a strong lead from the first quarter on.

By the end of the first half the score was 41-19, and 25 or 30 points were mine. I don't know if I'd missed a shot.

Coach McCord was glowing when we went downstairs to the locker room, and announced that the boys record at Franklin High School for points in a single game was 56, held by Crawford Alexander, who was in the crowd that night. He asked the team if they thought that I should break the record.

"Do you want to let him go for it?" McCord asked.

The team cheered.

I sat there stunned by the notion of it, but I didn't feel intimidated by the challenge. When I went back out on the floor, I just went back into basketball mode and didn't even think about the record.

The rest of the team was concentrating on getting me the ball. And when I had the ball, I shot it, even from far beyond what today would be the "three-point" line. In those days we just called it

Fred McMillan, left, keeps stats while Bobby roots from the bench. Next to Bobby are Albert Posnack and Jerry Whitehurst.

"downtown," and if I shot from downtown, I felt confident that I was going to make it.

Someone on the bench must have told someone in the stands what was going on, and it spread quickly through the gym and to the cheerleaders that Bobby Langley was going for the record. Every time I shot, the crowd yelled out my total. At the end of the third quarter I had 40 points. The fourth quarter started, it was a feeling that I never had before. The buzz in the gym seemed to grow as I sank jump shots, layups and long shots. I don't know exactly when I broke the record, but every time I'd hit a shot there was a roar. Finally the coach called a time out, and I sat out of the game for two minutes of rest before going back in.

It seemed like everything I shot that night went in, and I ended up with 69 points, 30 in the last quarter. My total points and quarter points both were school, Nashville Interscholastic League, and Mid-State records. That point total was seven shy of the state record.

When the game was over, the noise level stayed high. People streamed out of the stands and I got lifted up off the floor and paraded me around the gym. My life would never be the same. That game was remembered by many people for many years, and played a big part in my life and my career.

I have a pretty good memory about most things in my life. But for some reason, there are many details about the game I don't remember. But I do remember that when the game was over it seemed like it took me forever to get down to the dressing room. Nobody left the gym. When I got out of the shower and put my clothes on and came back up the steps, people started clapping.

My teammate Bubba McMillan, and his older brother, Fred, who had been helping Coach McCord with scoring and statistics during the game, told me to come with them. We hopped in their car and headed to the Gilco Drive-in. It was packed, and when I got out of the car there were people yelling, and cheering and screaming. When I went inside it was chaotic. I had never seen anything like it, and I had never felt like such a celebrity. Everybody wanted to talk about the game, and more people kept showing up. I went to Fred and Bubba's house, and then I went riding around with them. I finally got home at about 2 a.m.

People had been calling the house throughout the evening. My mother had never been to a basketball game and didn't know what they were talking about. She was hanging up on them. My father got home late from work and hadn't heard about the game either.

When I finally got to bed, I couldn't sleep, and lay awake until about 5 a.m. My father got up early and left. At about 7 a.m., I heard someone knocking at the door. My mother was up and I could hear a man asking "Is Bobby here?" She said "yes, he's asleep." She didn't invite him in, but came to the bedroom and said, "put your pants on, there's somebody who wants to see you about that old ball or something."

Coach David Johnston was standing on the doorstep with a copy of The Tennessean sports section with the headline "Franklin ace bags 69 points."
He shook my hand and said, "I just wanted to come by and tell you how proud I am of you."

We stood there outside, and I don't know what passed through his head, but I thought about my history with him, first as a little boy looking up to him as a high school athlete, and later when he let me play middle school baseball as an elementary student. Maybe he was thinking about it too: we both got a little bit emotional and misty eyed at that moment. It was a moment that I have cherished all my life.

Chapter 30: Fame

Coach Johnston was the first of many well-wishers that day. Later the newspaper called and wanted to arrange a photo shoot for the afternoon at Coach McCord's house.

Crawford Alexander, left, aims a fan at Bobby as Coach McCord looks on during a photo shoot for a sports story on Bobby's "hot streak." The photographer has used correction fluid to make it look like the fan is spinning.

To top it off, we had a charity game that night against Hillsboro, which turned out to be not such a good thing after the excitement of the night before and my lack of sleep. One of our starters, Wayne Irwin, wasn't there. I scored 30 points in that game, but we ended up losing by one.

A total of three teachers came up to me and said they were proud of me. The rest of them did not, maybe because I was a good basketball player and not much of a student. Mr. Sutton was proud, and said that my reputation had brought positive attention to the school.

Coach McCord was proud of me, but apparently had second thoughts during the weekend about having taken me out of the game for two minutes.

On Monday morning he said, "Bobby, I guess you realize that you did not play the whole game."

Knowing I had the Mid-state record all but wrapped up, he had taken me out of the game to give me some rest. But had he realized at the time that I was just seven points from breaking the state record for points in a single game, he would have let me play through.

Still, after my record-breaking night I became a target for all of our opponents. I usually had two players guarding me, but still managed 27 to 28 points per game. Individually, I was still having a good season, but we didn't always win. Our team wasn't as good as the team we had the year before, and with my ability to shoot, I had to carry a large part of the load on the offense.

A lot of kids go through high school without talking to the principal, but I began getting lots of calls to Principal Barry Sutton's office, and we ended up becoming good friends.

In late January I got a call to come to Mr. Sutton's office. Coach McCord was there. They told me that a guy from *The Nashville Tennessean* Sunday magazine "Showcase" wanted to come and do a story about me. The reporter planned to follow me around for a few days to my classes, go with me to practice, and be on the sidelines for a game.

It found the publicity kind of embarrassing, sometimes maybe even a little overboard.

The "Showcase" magazine article came out, and it was the cover story under the headline "Hotshot on the Hot Spot." But neither my dad nor my mother ever mentioned it.

My sister Mary Clair was getting up there in basketball herself, and finally my dad came to one or two of the games. I suspect that as her doting

Sandra West talks to Bobby in the halls of Franklin High School after his scoring record.

protector, he showed up just as much to make sure Mary Clair didn't go off with some boy after the game as he did to see her play.

During one of my games, hands and elbows were flying as usual, and somebody slapped me and broke my glasses down the middle. I had to change to my street glasses, which worked, but was not ideal. Coach McCord took the glasses after practice and said he would take care of it. A few days later I was practicing in my street glasses and Mr. Sutton called me in. Coach McCord was there. Mr. Sutton said "Bobby, we're going to take care of your glasses. You have done a lot for this school and we appreciate that."

Three days later I had new glasses.

In February, just before the district tournament, I got another call to come to the office and again Coach McCord was there with Mr. Sutton. *The Tennessean* sports department had called to tell me that I had been named to the 1959 Tennessean All-City basketball team. They wanted me to come to the newspaper office in Nashville to be measured and weighed, interviewed and photographed. Out of 250 players, they picked six. I was selected on the All-Midstate team, too.

With that honor, my dream and desire to be the best player in Williamson County had been met – maybe even exceeded.

Chapter 31: Crossroads

The end of the basketball season – and the end of that special, triumphant time in my life – was close. I felt that I had accomplished what I had set out to do.

But first was the Williamson County tournament, with West-Williamson/Fairview, Hillsboro, College Grove, Bethesda and Franklin. The championship came down to Franklin and Fairview, home of my impressive rival Eugene Pack. We ended up winning the tournament and for the second year, I was named MVP.

Nashville has its own Hillsboro high school in Green Hills, named for the pike that leads to the Williamson County Hillsboro. My brother, Hubert Lee was in the stands when we faced them, and the team was really after me. They tried to hold me back with double coverage, trash talk and fouls. I was dealing with it, but toward the end of the game one of the guys fouled me really hard. Hubert Lee jumped over people in the stands and came out on the floor and wanted to fight. His loyalty touched me,

Bobby goes up for a shot in a game against Nashville's Hillsboro High School.

but the scene embarrassed me. I just wanted to play.

As the end of the season approached I began to think bigger thoughts about why I was there, why I had my goal to be the best, and whether I had accomplished anything for anyone else. Reflecting on my own growing up watching high school students competing, I thought about the impact athletes have on those around them. There were young kids who came to the games and I could see them watching me and pointing to me from under the goal, and could hear them call my name. I would see them in town and they would want to talk about basketball. They would want to talk to me before the games. Even years later people younger than me would talk to me about those days, and how they used to come see me.

Growing up in Franklin I had many good role models myself, including high school athletes, like the baseball player who grew up and became Coach David Johnston. J.B. Akin and Ralph Brown from BGA inspired me with their kindness and their sense of duty to the school. Bull Mills even taught me a lot. And of course there was Coach McCord. Despite my disadvantages at home, I had learned integrity and decency and how to be polite. I had learned good sportsmanship. I played hard but I wasn't going to cuss people or rough them up. People noticed that.

I was happy about my accomplishments, but didn't have a clear view of what came next. I went to school to play basketball, and it was almost over.

The end for me came quickly in our second game of the district tournament. We got into a bracket with BGA. We won our first game, but faced BGA second. And like my first district tournament, when I was sophomore, they shut us down again. We lost by 10 or 12 points. For the third year in a row, I was named to the 22nd All-District team.

And that was it. It was over.

I don't think it bothered other seniors on the team like it bothered me. Most were looking forward to graduation and had a rough idea of where they were headed. But that was it for me.

Now that the season was over, student was my only role, and I still was doing my best.

But I was regularly breaking the school's closed campus rule. My dad had picked up a beat up '49 Chevrolet. Sometimes Mary Clair and I would drive the car to school. I made sure she had money for lunch, but sometimes that meant I didn't. On those days I had gotten into the habit of slipping off campus to drive home for lunch. After my trouble with the book report earlier in the year, Mary Clair had warned me that sooner or later someone was going to catch me.

Not long after the season I got another call to Mr. Sutton's office. I didn't know why and figured that I finally someone had reported me for leaving school. I walked into the office with a sense of dread, but it instantly turned to a feeling of shock and awe.

As I walked into Mr. Sutton's office a man got up out of his chair and turned to meet me. It was one of my all-time idols, Johnny Majors.

At the time he was practically every Tennessee boy's hero. As a UT football player, he had come in second in the Heisman voting in 1956, beaten by Paul Hornung. Now he was working as an assistant coach at UT, and as a recruiter. He had come to Franklin High to recruit my friends Ned Sullivan and Ray Dalton, but also to pass on a message to me. He wanted to tell Mr. Sutton that the UT basketball coach had my name on a top-prospects list, and he was told to tell me that. They knew I wasn't going to be able to go to college, but they wanted to tell me that they had noted my performance, and wanted to wish me luck. He then invited me to have lunch with him in the school cafeteria.

It was an honor to walk into the cafeteria with that superstar of the South, and it seemed like all eyes were on us as we had lunch.

I always had a good feeling in my heart about UT doing that. It impressed Mr. Sutton, too.

I ran track again that spring, and went to the state tournament with the two-mile relay team in Memphis.

Finally graduation was upon me, and for a change I wanted to do well on my final exams. When I walked across the stage to get my diploma, neither of my parents was there, but Mary Clair was there to cheer me on.

Chapter 32: Where will you play?

The day after graduation, Roy Apple and I went back to Kansas for the wheat harvest. And once again it was good to get out of town. It was hard for me to deal with the questions about where I was going to college, and who had offered me a scholarship.

"Where are you going to play ball next year?" was the number-one topic of small talk tossed my way. What do you say? How do you deal with that? There was a different feeling that was coming over me. School had been a rock in my shoe. Teenagers don't always think the right thing or do the right thing, especially those without the parental support or pressure to think things through, like grades and scholarships and the possibility of college.

My dad and I also had some problems during my senior year. Our family income had dropped when I quit the paper route, and my father and I had exchanged harsh words about that.

So I was glad to be going out West again, experiencing the change of scenery and environment. We spent about three months working the harvest, and as I did the work there I had a lot of time to think about how I had squandered my opportunity for a college education.

When I came home from the wheat harvest, the gravity of what I had done by avoiding difficult school work really hit me.

Roy Apple had graduated the year before and had worked for a year after graduation and saved his money to go to Middle Tennessee State in the fall.

Out of about 100 in our graduating class, about 30 went to college. Very few of the kids that came from families like ours and got their lunch free finished high school at all. It was because they got tired of dealing with the lack of spending money, lack of parental support, inability to dress right and difficulty of fitting in. I would think about that, whenever someone would tell me about someone who had quit school. It was always one of the kids who had gotten their lunch free. I made a point to keep up with them since we had a lot in common when we were young. Some of them eventually became very successful in business, or farming, or other fields.

At that time, I didn't see a clear path to success for myself. Our neighbor got me a job at Berry Wholesale Drug in Nashville. It was just a job to get me by.

I started seeing one of Mary Clair's good friends, Ann Larkins. She had come to live with J.W. and Ona Little because Ann's father had died and her mother was trying to get her family back in order. Ona Little and Ann were first cousins, and Ona's husband, J.W. Little, was from a large and well-known local family. Mary Clair and Ann were juniors at the time. Things seemed to be going well between Ann and I, but eventually she picked up on the fact that I wasn't doing much about my future and it wasn't long after that our relationship was history.

Ronnie was a little boy just starting school. Carolyn was still at home. Both J.T. and Hubert Lee had married and both were gone. I was still hanging around and my family still needed my help.

Being dumped by Ann Larkins kind of brought back memories of breaking up with Kathy Ashford because basically, it was for similar reasons. I didn't know where I was headed. I knew I had to find something.

I had graduated at 18, then turned 19 about a month later. For a young man of that age, the draft board was a reality, and the word "Vietnam" was beginning to creep into the newspapers.

I knew the lady at the draft board and she said both my name and Roy Apple's were coming up. Ronnie needed me and I was

Bobby Langley,
U.S. Army
National Guard

worried about being away too long. My father was still sick and couldn't give Ronnie the affection or attention he needed. So rather than join the regular Army for three years, I joined the Army National Guard. I had to go on active duty for about six months, and then go to drills for five more years.

I stayed in pretty good touch with my mom during my active duty training. But when I got back I was still at square one, not knowing what to do with my life. I had to find something. My first obligation still was to my family.

Chapter 33: A 'real' job

Mr. A.B. Thomas, who had owned the Gilco Drive-in in the '50s with his wife, Nell, and Milford Brown reopened Willow Plunge, after the Kinnard family had closed the popular swimming pool down for about three years. Mr. Thomas asked me if I wanted to work that summer as a lifeguard.

It was there I met Bill Morgan, who also had come to work at Willow Plunge. He knew people from a company called Geologic Associates in Brentwood that did foundation testing, soil sampling, and core drilling jobs all over the mid-South. Bill Morgan recommended me for a job, which became the first "real" job I had.

Today Brentwood is an upscale suburb of Nashville. But in those days it was a wide spot in the road between Melrose and Franklin. Singer Eddy Arnold had an office on the hill. The Pewitts had an Esso Station. There was Noble's Restaurant and a hardware store. A branch of the Harpeth National Bank shared a building with the post office. Geologic Associates had an office there, too.

These were the people who really taught me how to work. There was a lot to learn – things that I didn't learn in school. There were books to keep about our work, reports to write, measurements to take. There was a lot of physical labor for which I was well suited due to my recent Army training and my sports background.

For three years I traveled the country with Geologic Associates. Ironically, one of the first jobs I had was at Belmont College, where I had a scholarship that I could not accept because of my grades. I helped do the foundation testing for the Stribling Gymnasium, the college's new basketball arena.

We did a lot of work for NASA and for the Army's Redstone Arsenal in Huntsville, Alabama. We worked at the sites of future interstate highways, a dam, bridges, hospitals and buildings that are landmarks to this day.

I was gone quite a bit and would stay on jobs sometimes for a couple of months. But I would come home as much as possible to check on the family.

In about 1960 my parents moved into a brand new public housing project, a three-bedroom Franklin Housing Authority unit. It was another first for them: a fresh, new home.

My father's health had gotten worse and his drinking had escalated. He couldn't drive for the county anymore.

Mary Clair Langley set numerous records while playing basketball for the Franklin Lady Rebels.

Mary Clair was getting into her last year of basketball. She drew a crowd with her basketball skills. Mary Clair had broken several records, made all city twice, was in MVP voting, won just about every award for basketball that Franklin High School could give. After she graduated, she had gone off to Nashville Business College and played basketball there.

In 1963 I spent about eight months on a job in Hopkinsville, Ky., about 60 miles from Franklin. I rented an apartment there. One of the strangest days on that job was Nov. 22, the day President Kennedy was shot. Someone heard the news on a car radio and called the crew to gather around. We all listened to the broadcast for a while. Then everybody just walked off the job and started toward town. When we got to town there were no cars on the street, nobody walking around. Everybody had gone home to watch television.

When the Hopkinsville job was over, I got my mother and my little brother, Ronnie, to help me move my things out of the apartment. That was the first time in my mother's life that she had been out of the state of Tennessee.

In a strange parallel to the Belmont gymnasium job, I also ended up on the job at the University of Tennessee, Knoxville. We were doing foundation sampling for the Stokely Athletic Center, another basketball arena. At the time I remember thinking, "What's the Lord trying to tell me?"

Geologic Associates was a good job. I made enough money that I could help out my family, but because of the traveling, I couldn't help enough by just being there.

While I was on the road I spent a lot of time thinking about the kinds of jobs that paid people well who hadn't gone to college: the railroad, the Ford automobile glass plant, DuPont chemical, Nashville Electric Service, and the truck lines. It was hard to get on at most of those places.

I had some friends who had gone to work at Mason-Dixon Truck Lines, so I went there to fill out an application.

Jimmy Barr was the personnel director, and he recognized my name.

"Bobby Langley … are you the basketball player?" he asked.

That broke the ice: basketball once again had helped me move forward.

I told him that I wanted to work where I could be closer to home, and took some tests. As we talked I felt comfortable with him. And though he told me they didn't have anything available just then, I told him, "I'm going to worry you to death until you give me a job."

Every time I was close to a phone I'd call Mr. Jimmy Barr, and two or three months later, Mr. Barr had left a message at my mother's home that I could get on the "extra board," which meant that you got a shift when they needed you.

I accepted, and joined the union, and managed to get called in for a shift fairly regularly. Before long I was making pretty good money and got my own apartment in Franklin, on my own but close enough to check on my family a lot.

Chapter 34: 20 years of TB

By this time Carolyn, my youngest sister who shared many traits with our mother, had gotten married at 16 years old and left home, leaving just Ronnie at home with my parents. They had moved to a smaller apartment to save money on utilities.

Tyree poses with his wife, Ruby, three months before his death in 1965.

The year 1965 was my father's 20th year with tuberculosis. He was 56 years old and still was answering the phone at the cab stand. He was drinking more than ever and now had developed pancreatic cancer. Mary Clair knew, but he never told me.

One morning after I had got off from work, I went to the house to visit and my mother told me that my father had checked himself into the hospital. I had a bad feeling about it, but he had been sick my whole life, I didn't really recognize what was about to happen.

I went to the hospital to check on him, and he didn't look good and was down. I asked him if he wanted me to spend the night, or Mary Clair, but he said he didn't want anybody to spend the night. So I went home and I told my mother I'd check on him after I got off my midnight shift at the truck lines.

When I got back to the hospital the next morning, I walked into the room and started talking to him. A nurse had seen me going down the hall and followed me in and told me he had died overnight at about 2 a.m. He had told the staff not to summon the family. He didn't want to bother us with it.

They had tied a white cloth around his head to keep his mouth closed.

My reaction was mixed. I don't think he had ever told any of the kids that he loved them. He grew up in the Depression with a hard-nosed dad himself. I know he loved us, but it was not his way to talk about that. He lived a hard life. He never owned a home, never accumulated anything in his life, and never had money.

I told the people in the hospital that I would take care of the funeral arrangements and left.

When I got to my mother's house, Ronnie, 11, was having breakfast with her. After Ronnie went outside I told my mother that my father was gone. She didn't say anything. I think she knew what was going to happen when he told her that he was going to check himself into the hospital.

Ruby Irene Hammox Langley was 45 years old and had lost her husband. She'd only been with one man in her life and there wouldn't be another.

I left her where she could be by herself. Then I called my brothers, including my half-brother, William, to talk about making the funeral arrangements.

.

It was a sad time, but it wasn't really a sad time. My dad had never stopped drinking, and from time to time still flew into rages in which he insulted and even hit my mother.

Of all of us, Ronnie took it pretty hard. As the youngest, still at home, he and my dad had become close.

J.T., William and I went to the bank and borrowed the money to bury my dad at Mount Hope Cemetery. We decided not to ask the two girls to chip in.

Chapter 35: Basketball talk

My seniority finally came up at the truck line, and they took me off the extra board and gave me a regular shift. I bought myself a new 1965 Chevy Impala at Walker Chevrolet, the first time I ever had the money for a new car.

But just a short time later, there was a lull in the business and they started laying people off. Eventually it started getting closer to me. I didn't get laid off, but they did put me back on the extra board.

I was spending a lot more time around Franklin, and wherever I went, people still wanted to talk about basketball, even though by this time I was 25 years old. Mary Clair was 23, and it was the same for her, and for Hubert Lee, and for J.T. We had a lot of friends around town, and years later people still wanted to talk about those days, those games.

For a long time I still had to answer for not going to college, but eventually I didn't mind any more. I'd just tell people it was a long story and they'd accept that. Some people knew about my family and my sick father.

 In time I started to play golf a lot with John McCord, my friend from all the way back in junior high when he was one of the baseball pitchers. John also was a distant relative of Coach McCord, and like the coach, he also was a dedicated educator.

I also started to hang around at Dotson's Restaurant, one of those classic hometown places where all the politicians, Optimist and Lions Club guys held court. Most were people I had known all my life, including some that I'd served as a paper boy. When I got off at the truck lines, I would go there to drink coffee and to talk about sports.

I felt like for years I had lived with the stress of my upbringing and family situation. Now I was free of that, and I was known about town. All of my brothers and sisters were doing better and were able to help our mother and Ronnie. I had worked to get where I was and had a good feeling about myself. I was happy.

One night I was invited to a party thrown by some truck line co-workers from Williamson County. I met Lorene Reed there, a young woman from the Grassland area. I didn't know her, but she knew who I was from my basketball days, and from friends of friends. Personally, I was confident and in a good place, and it seemed like the two of us had some chemistry.

We started dating fairly frequently. She was attractive and had a good personality, and as young people tend to do, we started moving too fast. After knowing each other just for three or four months, we drove to Tupelo and got married.

Work continued to be scarce at the truck line, and I still was on the extra board working about three days a week. That gave me a lot of time to hang out in Dotson's.

That's where I was when one morning Paul Lankford was sitting across the table from me. Suddenly he stopped what he was doing and looked at me and said, "Bobby Langley, you need to go to work for me. You need to be in sales. I could line up all the people in this county that's your age, and you'd be the most well-known."

Paul Lankford was one of those football players at BGA that I had watched when I lived in Beasley Town. Now he was a junior partner in Morton Chrysler-Plymouth AMC on Hillsboro Road. He wasn't very old, and there certainly weren't people as young as me in the car business at the time.

"You think about that," he said. "You know a lot of people, you treat people nice, you've got to go to work for me."

I knew he was sincere, but I didn't know a thing about selling cars, so I let it ride. We didn't talk about it for a few weeks. But one morning I came in again and he asked me again.

My limited hours at the truck line were frustrating, so I told him to go ahead and ask Mr. Charlie Morton if I could work there.

I saw him a few days later and he told me that he had talked to Mr. Morton and Mr. Morton didn't want to hire me. I said that was fine, I had a job and had built up a bit of seniority there.

Still, it started bothering me. Mr. Morton had come to Franklin from West Nashville and married into Williamson County's well-known Sewell family. He probably knew where I was from, and my sports reputation likely didn't mean a whole lot to him. It started running through my mind what he must have thought and what he must have said. People from my background worked under cars in the service department, not around cars in the showroom.

A couple of months later I ran into Paul Lankford again. I was on another layoff. Paul said he would talk to Mr. Morton again. I saw him the next couple of days, and he said Mr. Morton wasn't sure he needed somebody, but he had agreed to give me a try.

I didn't resign from the truck line because if you were on the extra board and they called you, you didn't have to go. I just wanted to see how this car sales thing was going to work.

After being part of the union, going into the car business was a big step into the unknown. It was 100 percent commission. If you didn't sell anything, you didn't make anything, and that was a little bit scary. If I hadn't come to a point in my life where I was happy and not worried about this or that all the time, I probably never would have taken the chance.

Chapter 36: The perfect job

Very few people like a new job on the first day, and usually feel kind of awkward. But when I reported to the showroom at Morton's Chrysler Plymouth AMC on Hillsboro Road, I felt like I belonged there. I liked being around people. As I started to do the job, I knew that I was a natural. It was such an immediate good fit that it seemed God had looked down upon me and touched me.

Management had advertised that I was coming to work there and people responded, some coming in shopping for cars and others just stopping in to say hi. Most of the people who sold cars in Franklin were middle-aged men. I may have been the youngest salesman in town. But there was a whole generation right around my age who were in the car-buying market. There were people from high school who now were working after finishing college, and there were those who didn't go to college who were moving up in their jobs and getting married. The timing couldn't have been better for me.

It also was a good time for Chrysler and Plymouth, as NASCAR and Richard Petty had brought a lot of credibility to the brands.

In the first month I sold 10 or 15 cars. I could not believe that I had a job that I loved that much. I couldn't wait to go to work every day.

I had found my second calling in life, after basketball. On Nov. 16, 1967, Robert G. Langley Junior was born. We called him Bob, and having a baby filled us with excitement and joy. My good friend John McCord was the first to wish Bob junior well, paying tribute to his dad with the gift of a basketball that was almost as big as the baby.

John McCord was one of the first friends to show up with a baby gift for young Bob Langley: a basketball.

And though Lorene and I shared in those feelings of joy about Bob, both of us knew that we had moved too quickly into our relationship and that something was not quite right in our marriage. Between being a new father, and learning my profession, life was moving forward at a rapid pace.

I had no such doubts about the car business. Getting into it helped me overcome my regrets about not studying hard and not going to college. This was going to be my college. The business just took me over. A warm feeling came into my heart and just like that I resolved to learn the business from A to Z and be the best. I watched how buyers behaved. I watched how other people sold, how they talked to people. I started learning all about the cars and all about the financing.

As I watched other salesmen, I told myself, 'If they can do that, I can do that.'

One day Mr. Morton bought a car for $1,500, and just a few minutes later I sold it for $2,000.

Lewis Jackson, Sonny Harper and Bobby Langley pose after being named top salesmen for Harpeth Ford.

It wasn't very long until I could do it all: the contract, the banking, the titles. That's when I set another goal for myself: to have my own car business.

And after three years in the car business I couldn't imagine doing anything else … even coaching basketball. I had found my niche.

Sonny Harper was a dear friend of mine and was one of the best automobile salesmen in Williamson County. He was one of a few guys at Harpeth Ford who had been talking to me about coming to work there. I was doing well at Morton's and enjoyed it, but I knew that if I went to Harpeth Ford, I could learn even more about the business. They had trucks: pickups, farm trucks, work trucks.

They also had a big used car department and I knew that I needed to learn about that. So in 1969 I left Morton's and started selling Fords.

I'd like to say that having a child strengthened my marriage, but it didn't. Clearly we had moved too fast toward marriage in the first place, because in 1970, my marriage failed. Divorces never go very well when there is a young child involved, but we got through it. Bob's mother and I remained civil, and later even became friends again. I saw my boy a lot.

My work occupied my mind and helped me stay focused through the divorce. I worked very closely with Sonny Harper, and learned a lot from him. I also learned a lot from the owner of Harpeth Ford, R.C. Alexander. If working at Morton's was my college, working at Harpeth Ford was like getting my master's. And as time passed I thought more and more about going into the automobile business myself. I knew that was going to happen sometime down the road.

Mr. Charlie Morton was getting on in years and wanted to sell his business. He sold it to Joe Wheat and Jimmy Reynolds, who started trying to persuade me to come back there, and maybe buy in with them as a partner in the future. I wasn't really ready to change jobs again, but the more they talked about it, the more it seemed like a good opportunity.

But the timing couldn't have been worse. Not long after they took over Morton's the country experienced the first international oil crisis. Gasoline went from 32 cents to 62 cents a gallon. Wheat and Reynolds Chrysler Plymouth was stocked with big cars and muscle cars, and the business got off to a very shaky start. I had to go back up to Harpeth Ford.

Chapter 37: 'Let's do it'

Just as the car business found me over coffee at Dotson's, so did Mary Ann Pate of Eagleville, who had come from a sports-oriented family and who recognized me from my basketball days. We ended up having a lot in common and it wasn't too long before I started calling her "Sug," for sugar. And soon I was married again, but this time to the love of my life.

Bobby and his son Bob

We had a good partnership, and together saved money and bought a home on Bluegrass Drive. It felt like our marriage had momentum. The only disappointment was that we were not able to conceive children.

So after we were married for two or three years, and with the exception of regular visits from my son Bob, were childless, I decided that I had learned enough and was ready to go and start my own business.

I needed a loan to set up a used car business: to get a lot and office into shape, and to buy good cars to sell. I went to all the banks, and they all turned me down. Again I felt like it was because of my background. Franklin still was a small town where a person's pedigree, or lack thereof, was known. And unlike some young men my age who wanted to start a business, I didn't have a daddy who would back me up.

So I tried the Nashville banks, where I figured it would be all about business, but they all told me no as well.

Since I couldn't get the financing to start my own business, I knew that I probably needed to go work in the car business in Nashville to build up my reputation and get some connections. I needed to know people where I could go buy good used cars in the future for my business. Bobby Wiley, a Franklin guy and childhood friend, worked at Crown Ford, so I went and worked there for a year and I did well, and I loved it again. They offered me a manager job but I turned them down because I knew I wasn't going to stay. I was learning what I wanted to learn and meeting people.

After the year at Crown Ford I found another lot to rent that seemed ideal, I felt like I needed a partner. Bobby Wiley was honest so I asked him to join me. But even with the two of us involved, I went to the banks again, and again they turned me down.

My wife and I had owned our home for four years, since 1972. After getting rejected again by the banks, I told her that my only solution was to sell our home and take the equity out of it and start the business.

She believed in me, and her reply was one I will never forget.

"Let's do it," she said.

It took me 10 years – almost to the day – to get my own place: 1966 to 1976, 10 years from the time I told myself I was going to have my own business. Sug and I moved into an apartment.

Bobby Wiley had to sell his house, too.

We opened up a used car and truck operation on Hillsboro Road and named in Car Country. Our specialty was the "second car," and in those days a good-looking, reliable used car could be had for an average of $1,500.

The year I had spent at Crown Ford helped me a lot. I had made a lot of connections with wholesalers and other people in the car business. We had found a "sweet spot" in the auto business. I was running the roads just about every day and buying cars. It was going well. Sales were great – we could barely get enough cars.

As naïve as it was, I was oblivious at the time to the fact that many people thought automobile dealers were crooks, cheats and liars. After all, as I grew up in Franklin, the car dealers were all honorable people, church elders, members of the Rotary, Little League coaches and Scout leaders. The town still was too small for a cheat or a liar to last very long in a business like that.

Our success right off the bat was a dream come true. I had put my time in to learn my profession, and now I had the business on my terms: treat people right.

Bobby Wiley and Bobby Langley pose across from Car Country.

Business remained brisk, and was going so well that Mary Ann and I were able to buy another home after just a short time in the apartment, this time south of town in a new subdivision called Redwing Farms.

And after two years on Hillsboro Road we decided that we needed more room. We had a chance to get our own property, so we made a deal with Mr. Robert Sanders for his place on south Columbia Avenue, not far from my high school home on Fairgrounds Street. It needed a lot of remodeling, which we did.

Moving the business wasn't the biggest change in my life. Despite the medical tests and examinations, and conclusions by doctors that it wasn't going to happen, Sug walked into my office one day and told me she was pregnant. John Pate Langley, my second son, was born in 1978.

The new location for the business was challenging. Traffic wasn't as good there as it was on Hillsboro Road. If that wasn't enough, there was another round of dramatic oil price increases. The economy went south under President Jimmy Carter, and interest rates shot up. The 21 percent interest on our building was eating us alive.

We decided to sell the property, and the people who owned the back part of the lot bought it. After it was sold we dissolved our partnership. Bobby Wiley went off on his own. I leased the property back and took on Sonny Harper as a partner. Bobby Wiley kept the Car Country name and we called our place Harper and Langley.

In the early '80s, after the election of Ronald Reagan, business took off again. And one day Sug came in to the office and told me that she was pregnant again. Lindsey Clair Langley was born in

November, 1981, and was named Clair after my sister. We felt joyful and blessed.

With an improving economy and more going on around Franklin, Harper and Langley Auto Sales started off with a bang, just like Car Country had.

I loved my partner, Sonny Harper, like a brother. But as my kids grew older and I felt more confident about my ability to run and finance things myself, I wanted to be in business on my own. By 1986 I felt like I was ready, and braced myself for one of the hardest things I ever went through. The day finally came that I had to tell Sonny Harper that I wanted to buy him out.

BOBBY LANGLEY AUTO SALES

1504 Columbia Avenue
Franklin

LOCALLY OWNED
& OPERATED

790-9487

"Quality for Less"

HOURS: Monday-Friday 8:00 a.m.-6 :00 p.m.
Saturday 8:00 a.m.-3:00 p.m.

Mary Ann, Pate, Lindsey, & Bobby Langley

Bobby Langley Auto Sales advertises the family and the slogan "Quality for Less."

It broke my heart to tell him, and I could tell that he was crushed, too.

The business now was called Bobby Langley Auto Sales. I redid the buildings again. Business still was good. I had cultivated a chain of wholesalers and regularly would lock up the office and go on buying trips.

Chapter 38: My own boss

In 1986 and 1987 Franklin hadn't really started growing yet: at least, not the kind of growth it was about to see that ended up changing transforming the town from small town to Nashville suburb.

Gov. Lamar Alexander and General Motors had announced that they were going to locate their plant for the Saturn automobile in the area, the state had announced that they would build State Route 840 through the southern part of the county, in part to serve the growth that Saturn would bring. And finally, American Airlines announced that they were locating a hub in Nashville. Those three big things lined up to change the face of Middle Tennessee.

Ronnie, Carolyn, Hubert Lee, Mary Clair, J.T. and Bobby pose with Ruby Irene Hammox Langley.

It was a good time for the automobile business, and domestic cars were my bread and butter. The Olds Cutlass was popular as were Ford and Chevy pickups, and a lot of Chrysler products.

My kids were doing well in school, my wife and I were happy with our lives. Bob junior had moved to Nashville with his mother, but he and I were really tight. He would spend weekends and summers with us, and spend time in my office and ride with me on car-buying trips.

More than once Sug and I tried to get my mother to move in with us. J.T., Mary Clair and Carolyn all wanted her to get to know their children, and we suggested that she spend months or maybe a year living with each of us. But she didn't want to leave her home at the Franklin Housing Authority, where she felt secure and settled.

My siblings mostly were doing well. Mary Clair was managing the office for Middle Tennessee Electric Membership Corp. in Franklin. Carolyn was still married, and by then had three children. J.T. was doing well and had a hardware sales territory in Middle Tennessee.

My youngest brother Ronnie was on his second tour in Germany with the U.S. Army, along with his wife, Sheila, and daughter,

Bobby Langley, upper right, coached the county champion Lady Rebels rec league basketball team featuring Lindsey Langley, lower right. Mickey Hinkle, upper left, was the assistant coach.

Melanie.

Hubert Lee was married and had a son, but his life was still a bumpy road.

There's nothing in the world like working for yourself. I'd seen the stress that having a boss puts on people. Even though running your own business can be stressful, I think working for yourself is a lot healthier. I was happy to be working for myself not for the money, but for peace of mind.

I had a lot of peace of mind at that time, and I tried to be the parent that I had always wanted to have. I made it a point to be being involved with my children's lives. I encouraged them to be in sports, like Little League with my son and softball with my daughter. I got involved in coaching as well. I was an older parent, but I was loving being involved, because when I was a kid I didn't have that.

Chapter 39: Back to the BGA gym

I turned 50 years old in 1990, which also was the year my half-brother, William, passed away. GM-Saturn put out their first car from the new plant in Spring Hill. Developers were buying up land, including the Holland-Langley farm in Spring Hill, which now is a subdivision. A new mall went in north of downtown Franklin.

But lots of people still stopped by to talk, and a lot brought copies of old stories of my basketball days they had cut from the newspapers. I accepted all of them and would store the papers in a desk in a back office at the dealership.

My son Pate was finishing Middle School, and he tested and got into Battle Ground Academy on the old campus near where I grew up.

It was a little emotional for me sometimes to be on that campus where I had spent so much time growing up. Pate was a little behind the other students, and like me he wasn't the best student in the world, but he was a good all-around athlete. He played B-team basketball and became a starter in baseball. His sophomore year he became the top hitter on the baseball team. He also was on the basketball team, and in his sophomore year he made the varsity. His junior year he became a starter on the basketball team, and his team won the district and regional tournaments at the end of the season. During the awards ceremony at the Regionals they called out his name for the All-Region team. Sug and I were there.

Jesse Turner, one of the guys I grew up with in Beasley Town, also had his son in BGA. During the years we lived close to the campus, blacks did not go to BGA.

We had lived with segregation, and though it did seem wrong at the time, it also was normal. But BGA, Franklin, and the whole United States had come a long way since then. By 1996 it was a national shame.

Now both of our sons were playing together in the gym that both of us had watched being built and now was about to close as BGA prepared to move to a new campus. Jesse Turner and I, who had played together on that old campus, were sitting together in the stands.

Pate Langley plays basketball in 1997 at the Battle Ground Academy gym where his father practiced as a boy.

"Jesse, nobody would believe this," I said. "We are sitting here 50 years later from the day we met each other in 1946, and out on the floor our sons, a black boy and a white boy, are playing together, Lamont Turner and John Pate Langley."

Those two boys could never dream how proud we were that they were teammates.

Pate graduated in 1997 from BGA, and went on to graduate from the University of Tennessee. Lamont Turner ended up graduating from Vanderbilt.

My daughter Lindsey shined, too. In Middle School she was an honor roll student, was part of the student council, was a cheerleader and played softball. She continued at that pace in high school.

Chapter 40: Belated honor

Forty years after my own achievements as a high school basketball player, people still were coming up to me to talk about those days, and how it was possible for me to score 69 points in one game.

The most surprising recounting of my high school exploits came on a cold day in February, 1998. Business was slow. A man whom I recognized but couldn't quite place walked into my office and introduced himself.

"I'm Doug Crozier," he said. "I am the principal at Franklin High School. I want to talk to you."

I didn't have a clue what this man wanted.

"I've come to tell you that before the basketball season is over, we're going to retire your jersey at Franklin High School."

I was stunned.

"I'm sorry that this wasn't done years ago," he said. "You did so much for the school."

I couldn't even speak. I left him sitting there by himself and walked to the back office. I got very emotional and my mind flew through the years. I thought about a thousand things in a matter of two minutes. My eyes were watery.

I didn't know what to say. I went back out there and told Mr. Crozier that Mary Clair's jersey should be retired, too.

He said mine was going to be, and it would be soon, at a Friday night game. He said he would be back in touch.

"By the way," he said, "what was your number?"

I said it was 22. Then I shook his hand and thanked him, and he left.

For a while I just sat there and enjoyed the moment. I didn't call anybody, I just sat there alone, thinking about the past and about how I got to where I was at that time. I'd had some proud moments in my life. I thought about all the boys I grew up with, all those old gyms I'd played in, and playing pickup ball at the County Center with black boys who were older and taller than I was. I thought about Mary Clair, and how she had followed a similar path to mine through basketball. I thought about Coach David Johnston, who first gave me a chance to play sports as an elementary student and who years later had been the first to congratulate me the morning after I set the scoring record in high school. I thought about Coach Ernest McCord, who shaped my talent and influenced my life so much as a mentor and a friend. Coach McCord had passed away in 1989. I thought about all the people who had helped me through life.

I finally did call my wife. Later on that night she would call and tell the children.

My head was still spinning the next day. I didn't go on and play college ball, and it really made me wonder, "am I worthy of this?"

Principal Crozier and the Franklin High staff announced their intentions to retire my jersey. *The Tennessean*, the *Franklin Review Appeal*, and the *Williamson Leader* all interviewed me. It was in the paper the morning of the day they were going to do it. My phone started ringing at 6:30 a.m. I was late for work, but when I unlocked the office, the phone was ringing there, too. One of the first calls I got was from Mr. Barry Sutton, principal of Franklin High School in my day.

Bobby's eyes mist up as he walks off the court at Franklin High with Mary Ann after his jersey number was retired. Mary Clair is at left.

My mother, Ruby Irene, by now had moved out of the Franklin Housing Authority projects and into a nursing home. I went over there at the end of the day on Friday to talk to her. She said lots of people had been coming in to congratulate her about her boy and she asked, "What does all that mean?"

I said what she had said to me so many times, "Oh, mama, it's just something about that old ball."

I thought about how proud I was to have seen my son, Pate, named to the All-Region team, and to see my daughter, Lindsey, on the honor roll. I was sad that she couldn't enjoy the moment with me then, and never could as I was playing basketball in school. But she had never gone to ball games. She had never read about sports in the papers. It was just another thing that she couldn't understand.

I understood my mother. And I loved her and appreciated what she went through for us.

I cried for her that day. As a father I had experienced pride and joy in the accomplishments of my children. I was sad that my mother could not relate to the accomplishments of her own.

My brothers and sisters were excited, though. Mary Clair called me and we went out to the school together that night for the ceremony. I was worried about having to make a speech because I knew I would get choked up about it.

My wife, my children and my brothers and sisters all went out to the middle of the floor. Both teams were lined up to congratulate me. Channel 4 and Channel 2 were there from Nashville. Some of my teammates were there.

My number 22 jersey, and my picture, ended up in a case outside the gym.

I stayed on a high for a long time. For months afterward people continued to congratulate me and talk to me about it. There seemed to be a lot of people who still remembered the excitement of those days 40 years past.

Bobby's jersey hangs in the hallway of Franklin High School.

The next few months the health of my mother was up and down, and she was feeling stress. The woman whose life was years of make do, hard work and few pleasures had become fussy. She complained about things big and small.

On a July morning about 5 a.m. my wife answered the phone and passed it to me. It was Claiborne Hughes nursing home. My mother had died of a massive heart attack. They assured me that she had suffered no pain.

She had, however, had a rough life, including the 33 years since my father had died that she spent without a partner.

She finally rejoined Tyree in Mount Hope Cemetery. The day of her funeral was a sad one for her six children, because all of us knew that her road through life had not been an easy one.

Of all her children, I think I had spent the most time through the years talking to her, getting her to open up and tell me about how she met my father and how their courtship and early married life progressed.

I knew on the day of her funeral that I wanted to tell the story of her journey, and I stood beside her grave for a long time that day reflecting on many of the things that I finally set down here.

Chapter 41: Telling the story

Time does fly by. Suddenly it was the year 2000, a year of many milestones for the family.

In February of that year Mary Clair got a call from Doug Crozier who told her that they were going to retire her basketball jersey, just like mine had been.

Mary Clair Langley was the second Langley sibling to have a basketball jersey number retired at Franklin High School.

She acted like it wasn't a big deal and that she wasn't excited, but I know she was.

The night of her ceremony there was a big crowd including many of her teammates and her coach, Howard Gamble. Representatives of her class came out and presented her with a bouquet of flowers.

Hubert Lee wasn't at her ceremony, nor was he at mine. He had begun to have a lot of health problems, including a mild stroke.

And then in May of 2000, at age 62, Hubert Lee died of a massive stroke.

His was a sad story. He was well liked when he was young and had a lot of ability, but never accepted his limits and spent a lot of his life frustrated and bitter.

Hubert Lee's son, Randall Tyree Langley, went to Page High School, as did my daughter, Lindsey Clair. His son, like Hubert Lee, was a good athlete.

My daughter also was playing sports and was very active in everything at Page High School. She was president of the student body, captain of the cheerleaders, was involved in the school plays, sang in the chorus and was in a lot of school programs. She graduated from Page that year, just before I turned 60 years old.

.After I turned 60 I noticed how much the town had changed. It wasn't the same place as it was in 1990. It wasn't even the same place as it was in 1995.

Mary Ann, Pate, Bob, Bobby and Lindsey are all smiles during a Christmas celebration in 1996.

I loved Franklin all my life. The town had nurtured and shaped me. For all who had snubbed me because of my background, there were many more who offered me friendship and help and acceptance. For a while, Franklin put me on a pedestal as a high school sports hero. And for a long time after that, people remembered me as someone who they could be proud of as one of their own.

But now every once in a while a salesman or someone would stick his head into my office and asked me where I got the miles turned back on my cars, which was an insult to me. For most of my run as an independent car dealer I had people's trust. It was only in the previous few years that I began to feel like more people I ran into had this negative stereotype of used car dealers, including me.

Having had a good name for so long in town and dealing with people I knew and the children of people I knew, it really bothered me to feel looked down upon as a businessman. People who didn't even know

Bobby Langley announces to the world his intention to retire.

me didn't trust me. They had moved here from bigger towns and had opinions of people with businesses like mine. The scales seemed to be tipping toward that, and away from the good reputation that I had built all my life. I began to get the feeling that my time had passed me by.

As we got to the end of the summer I began to talk to my wife about retiring, and that fall we made the decision to do that. I felt like I had been a success and I wanted to leave on my own terms, with a business that was still successful and while I was healthy.

I made a deal on the property, sold all the cars on the lot, and closed the business. On Oct. 1, 2000, Bobby Langley Auto Sales was no longer there.

Lindsey poses with her dad at her graduation from the University of Tennessee, Knoxville.

One of the last things I did as a businessman was walk downtown. Closing my business was an emotional thing, and I was in a reflective mood as I took a walk around the square. I saw a few people I knew, but not many. By the year 2000 I could walk around the square in Franklin on any given day and not see anybody I knew. But that day I was enjoying the moment, and chose a place to sit down and think about the path that I – Ruby's boy – had taken and where it had led. I didn't owe anybody anything. My kids were doing well. Lindsey was in college and Pate was just about finished. My son from my first marriage, Bob, was living in New York City using his musical talents in ministry at Times Square Church. I felt that I had found success in my marriage, success as a parent, and success in my occupation. What more could I ask for?

Franklin had changed a lot, but I still loved the place. There was a lot of my past in that town square, like the cab stand where my father worked, the newspaper office where I rolled papers for so many years, the streets where I rode bicycles and scooters to deliver the papers. Over the years there had been issues about class, but overall people in this town had been good to us, and good to me.

After sitting for a while on a bench in the square, I got in my car and I went home a happy man.

For a while I didn't do much except enjoy retirement, play golf, and enjoy my family and friends.

Oldest son Bob Langley and Shar Pacheco – later his wife – watch the Macy's Thanksgiving Day Parade in New York.

My first born son, Bob junior, was the first of my children to marry. He was living in New York City at the time of the 9/11 attack, and went ahead with his wedding a month later to Shar Pacheco on Oct. 13, 2001, in a small town 60 miles up the Hudson River from the city. It was a happy time for the family.

After a while I felt compelled to tell the story of my family, and the story of a part of Franklin and a time that had been left out of most of the local historic accounts.

For many years my brothers and sisters and I thought we had to live with shame. Our father was the way he was: a drinker, a poor provider. Our mother was the way she was: intellectually limited. Our family was poor.

When I started writing about the times, places and characters of old Franklin, and in one of my first stories – about Beasley Town – I made the statement that we were on welfare.

After that story was published in the newspaper I felt kind of like an alcoholic admitting his problem. The shame was lifted off my shoulders and I felt free.

The kids who played together in Beasley Town, Bobby, Jesse Turner, Robert Junior Williams, Mary Clair and J.T., reunite near the site of their childhood homes at Carter and Granbury streets.

The way our parents were was part of the history of the South and the legacy of the Great Depression. The fact that Papa John and Pinky Belle were first cousins was another part of life at that time, and our mother was the product of that.

Our family, and my brothers and sisters, were woven into the history of a small town in the South, and the good things about that environment and the good people around us are what saved us from what could have kept us poor, and left us feeling angry about it.

Franklin is all about history, and markers around town tell the story of the Civil War Battle of Franklin, of fine old homes and of the history of education. After my story about Beasley Town was published in the newspaper, I talked to Heritage Foundation historian Rick Warwick about that chapter of local history: about diversity and integration before it was the law of the land, and

Bobby and J.T. pose with historian Rick Warwick at the dedication of the Beasley Town historic marker. The old Battle Ground Academy campus is in the background.

On Sept. 20, 2005 we put up a historic marker for Beasley Town that was dedicated in memory of my mother, Ruby Hammox Langley, the uneducated daughter of poor tenant farmers.

Two years later my beloved sister, Mary Clair, died in Nov. 1, 2007 at 65 years old. The great athlete had never been sick in her life, but had suddenly suffered a massive stroke. She had spent a life dedicated to her church, the Jehovah's Witnesses.

Chapter 42: Ruby's Angels

My brother J.T. and I were in the habit of going on long walks together in the parks and along the streets around Franklin, talking about the world, the town, our friends and our families.

One day we were talking about some of the hard times we had faced as a family when J.T. said to me, "you know, it was amazing what our mother did and how she handled the situation growing up with us."

I said, "Yes it was. How did she handle that all those years with all those kids and no education, and no way to make a living other than welfare and us helping with paper routes?"

He stopped me and said, "You don't know? You don't know how she done all that all those years?"

"No," I said. "How did she work that out? How did she do that being like she was?"

He said, "Well, Ruby's angels. She had three or four angels that were with her all her life from the time she was born."

"Are you serious," I said.

"Oh yeah. They watch over us, too: Ruby's angels."

J.T. wasn't the type of guy to say things like that, but he did, and he meant every word of it.

Epilogue

A generation after the children of Ruby and Tyree Langley grew up, tenant houses and run down shacks, poverty and welfare, alcohol and domestic violence are part of my family's history, not our present.

But there is no shortage of young people today growing up in similar conditions: short of lunch money, lacking stylish clothes, parents missing from teacher conferences and special events, in need of their own angels.

My mother may have been watched over by angels, but it was also human angels who helped make difference in my life. I hooked on to role models and observed how they conducted their lives and what they stood for, from student athletes of good character to coaches and teachers and ordinary working men and women. People helped lead me to the loves in my life, including sports and my career. But it was the way they led their lives that made the biggest difference in mine, beginning with my beloved grandfather, Papa John Wesley Hammox.

We do not remember him for marrying his first cousin, but for his kindness and support through the years for his children and grandchildren. Papa John was Ruby's first angel.

I named my second son, John Pate Langley, for Papa John, and for some of the other human angels who brought light to my life, such as my brother, J.T., my business partner, John D. "Sonny" Harper, and my close friend John McCord.

And now my first grandson, John Tucker Langley, has been named for Papa John. Cate and John Pate Langley's son was born Dec. 18, 2010, at Baptist Hospital in Nashville, great, great grandson of John Hammox.

There's no doubt in my mind that Ruby's Angels will follow him, too.

Bobby Langley holds John Tucker Langley as his father, Pate, looks on.

Acknowledgments

Mary Ann Langley (Sug), my wife; and my children Bob Jr., Lindsey Clair and John Pate are the air that I breathe. Without them I am nothing. I have said many times in my life that my greatest joy has been the time that I have shared with Sug and our children.

It has been difficult to write about my mother, Ruby, and her family. I have recounted the facts about her limited understanding of the world, due both to natural factors and to her isolation as a child. I have written about the handicaps of her siblings. I have done so with much love and respect for my mother and all of her family, of whom I gained understanding through the years. I learned that along with their limitations they also had gifts of compassion and devotion to family, as well as special skills. My Aunt Dorothy, for example, was a gifted photographer. Her treasured photographs are in this book illustrating my early family life. The Hammox and Fitts families did a lot for my family over the years, and for that I am grateful.

Equally, the Holland and Langley families, including the "second family" of my grandfather, Papa Gene, are precious to me. His second wife, Mama Lela, was the only grandmother I knew. She was an angel who came to my widower grandfather and brought him more children and brought me more aunts and uncles and cousins. Her loving influence on those children made them special people. I always wished that we could have spent more time together, and I feel great love for them as well.

I will never forget how a young Franklin businessman, Paul Lankford, saw something in me and led me to my second love in my life after sports: my career in the auto business. Lankford brought me into the career that allowed me to live the American dream.

This book would not have been possible without the encouragement of Hudson Alexander, who listened to my stories and urged me to put them on paper. Nor would it be possible without my editor, Mark Cook, who listened, learned, observed and understood in a way that I never thought anyone who hadn't seen or lived these things could.

The Lord told his disciples to "Be not afraid." This book is for all the people in the world who have lived in fear, as I did, before I knew myself and found faith. It was role models who led me to know myself and find my loves in life, and I hope that all those who live with fears can find their own role models and inspiration.

Finally, this book is about the goodness of the people of Williamson County, Tennessee – my home. I love every one of you.

Bobby Langley, Feb. 28, 2011

Index

Car Country **131, 132, 134**
Carter, Jimmy **133**
Cascade Plunge **74**
Casey Tobacco Warehouse **88**
Chester, J.B. **44**
Claiborne Hughes **142, 144**
Clara Dotson's Snack Shop and Restaurant **61**
Clouse, Herbert **77, 78**
College Grove High School **90, 94, 109**
Columbia Central High School **81, 82, 90, 91**
Cook, Jimmy **49**
County Center **59, 63, 73, 84, 141**
Crown Ford **131, 132**
Crozier, Doug **140, 141, 145**
Culleoka High School **82**
Dalton, Ray **65, 66, 88, 111**
David Lipscomb University **100**
Davis, Joey **94**
Dixon, Goldie **38**
Dotson's Restaurant **123, 124, 130**
Duplex community **9, 18, 20**
Ellison, Early **38**
Fairgrounds Street **62, 64, 78, 133**
Fitts, Charlie **33, 35**
Fitts, Richard **33, 35**
Five Points **3, 6, 53**
Forrest, Nathan Bedford **8, 85**
Fort Campbell **21, 94**
Fourth Avenue Church of Christ **37**
Fox, Tom **6**
Franklin Elementary School **3, 6, 39, 47, 54**
Franklin High School **43, 54, 71, 74, 107, 143, 145**
Franklin Housing Authority **117, 136, 142**
Franklin Junior High School **47, 59, 62, 64, 65, 66**
Franklin Review Appeal **141**
Franklin Training School **63**

Frazier, Donald **86, 88**
Frost, Ken **81**
Gamble, Howard **145**
Garrett, William **74**
General Motors **135, 138**
Geologic Associates **116, 118**
Georgetown College **100**
Gilco Drive In **73, 82, 103, 116**
Grand Ole Opry **49**
Hammox, Dorothy **39, 13, 27, 85, 156**
Hammox, James **13, 27, 85**
Hammox, John Wesley **11, 12, 13, 15, 17, 18, 20, 25, 26, 28, 30, 31, 33, 34, 35, 85, 150, 153**
Hammox, John Wesley Jr. ("Bug") **13, 27, 85**
Hammox, Pinky Belle Fitts **11, 12, 18, 27, 35, 150**
Hammox, Vester **13, 27, 85**
Hammox, Wesley Eugene ("Sonny") **85**
Hard Bargain **56**
Herbert Shell **73, 84**
Heritage Foundation of Franklin and Williamson County **151**
Hillsboro High School, Nashville **88, 99, 105, 109**
Hillsboro High School, Williamson County **90, 109**
Hampshire High School **99**
Harper, Sonny **128, 129, 133, 134, 153**
Harpeth Ford **128, 129**
Hinkle, Mickey **136**
Holland, Cynthia Clair **9, 21**
Holland-Langley farm **69, 138**
Holland, Mattie Glenn **8**
Holland, Sophia **9**
Holland, Tyree Lafayette **8**
Hopkinsville, Ky. **117, 118**
Hornung, Paul **111**
Howard, Gayle **5, 6**
Inman, Robert **92**
Inman, Wayne **92**

Langley, Margaret **29**
Langley, Marie **29**
Langley, Mary **69**
Langley, Mary Ann Pate ("Sug") **130, 133, 156, 131, 136, 138**
Langley, Mary Clair **20, 22, 31, 32, 38, 44, 57, 59, 66, 88, 94, 95, 97, 107, 111, 112, 114, 117, 120, 123, 135, 136, 140, 141, 143, 145, 150, 151, 155**
Langley, Melanie **137**
Langley, Nellie Joe **69**
Langley, Pate **133, 138, 139, 142, 148, 153, 154, 156**
Langley, Patsy **29**
Langley, Perry **10, 25, 26, 28, 29, 33**
Langley, Polly **10, 91**
Langley, Randall Tyree **146**
Langley, Ronnie Merrell **69, 94, 114, 115, 118, 120, 121, 124, 135, 136, 155**
Langley, Ruby Irene Hammox **1, 11, 12, 13, 15, 17, 18, 20, 24, 30, 35, 39, 62, 69, 78, 85, 120, 121, 135, 142, 148, 151, 152, 153, 154, 155**
Langley, Shar Pacheco **149**
Langley, Sheila **136**
Langley, Thomas ("Buck") **69**
Langley, Tyree Eugene **8, 9, 10, 11, 12, 13, 15, 16, 17, 19, 20, 24, 32, 33, 39, 69, 78, 85, 120, 144, 153, 155**
Langley, Vivian **29**
Langley, William ("Mum") **10, 29, 30**
Lankford, Paul **124, 125, 156**
Larkins, Ann **114**
Lawrenceburg High School **81**
Lewisburg High School **99, 101**
Lee, Dorothy **62**
Linden High School **81**
Little, J.W. **114**
Little, Ona **114**
Lofton, James **44**

Majors, Johnny **111**
Mangrum, Kenneth **94**
Mason-Dixon Truck Lines **118, 128, 123**
Maury County **15, 49**
McCord, Coach Ernest **86, 87, 88, 89, 90, 92, 94, 95, 97, 99, 100, 101, 103, 104, 105, 106, 107, 108, 110, 111, 123, 141**
McCord, John **64, 123, 126, 127, 153**
McLemore, Reuben ("Duck") **17, 22**
McMillan, Bubba **66, 103, 104**
McMillan, Fred **103, 104**
Melrose **74, 116**
Middle Tennessee Electric Membership Corp. **136**
Middle Tennessee State University **100, 113**
Miller, Bill **54**
Miller, Tommy **54**
Mills, L. I. ("Bull") **47, 54, 55, 110**
Montgomery Bell State Park **75**
Moody's Tire **53**
Morgan, Bill **116**
Morton, Charlie **125, 127, 129**
Morton Chrysler Plymouth AMC **124, 126, 128, 129**
Mount Carmel Church **19**
Mount Hope Cemetery **122, 144**
Mount Pleasant High School **99**
Nashville Banner **53, 91**
Nashville Business College **117**
Nashville Electric **98, 118**
Nashville Interscholastic League **100, 103**
Natchez **4, 41, 63**
Natchez High School **63**
Ogilvie, Rufus **11, 12, 18**
Pack, Eugene **90, 109**
Parman School **30, 32, 34**
Petty, Richard **126**
Pewitt Farm **34**
Porky's Store **41, 73**

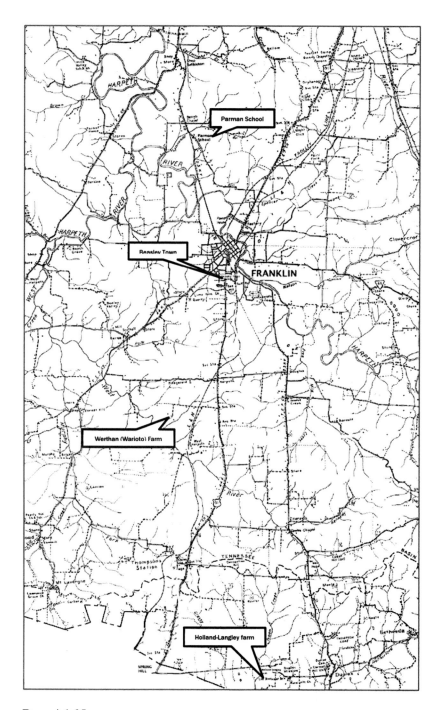